THE PROP BUILDER'S
MASK-MAKING
HANDBOOK

THE PROP BUILDER'S
MASK-MAKING
HANDBOOK

THURSTON JAMES

Betterway Publications, Inc.
White Hall, Virginia

Published by Betterway Publications, Inc.
P.O. Box 219
Crozet, VA 22932
(804) 823-5661

Cover design by David Wagner
Photographs by the author, except as noted
Typography by Typecasting

Library of Congress Cataloging-in-Publication Data

James, Thurston
    The prop builder's mask-making handbook / by Thurston James.
        p.   cm.
    Includes bibliographical references and index.
    ISBN 1-55870-167-2: $27.95. — ISBN 1-55870-166-4 (pbk.): $17.95.
    1. Mask making. I. Title.
TT898.J36   1990
731'.75 — dc20   90 – 38115
                                                                           CIP

Printed in the United States of America
0 9 8 7 6 5 4 3 2 1

My wife has been helpful in the last eight years as I was working on these books on prop building. Of course, she exhibited the patience that a spouse must, during the hours their partner sits at the typewriter. And she willingly waived the weekends and holidays that could have been spent in vacation in order that the work continue.

But my wife has done more. Thirty years ago, as we were courting, she cooperated unselfishly when I suggested that she allow me to make a casting of her face. Straws were lovingly placed in her nose and her face was gently piled with plaster. Positive and negative copies were made with fiberglass, and these relics were preserved.

The following photograph reveals my wife's face, cast in nine of the mask-making materials demonstrated in this book.

(Bottom row, left to right) Papier-mâché; cloth and glue; Celastic; and vacuum-formed styrene. (Top row, left to right) Friendly Plastic; Hex-a-cel; latex; neoprene; and leather.

For her patience, understanding, tolerance, for her love and the five children we reared, and for giving me her face when I needed it, I dedicate this book to my wife Rosella.

ACKNOWLEDGMENTS

I want to thank Pip Taillefer, artist, leather sculptor, and currently scenic artist at The Department of Theater UCLA for teaching me the basic techniques of leather shaping.

I want to thank Dan Jue for conducting a leather mask making workshop in the winter of 1988. He shared the techniques of leather mask making with several students and myself that he had acquired the previous summer in Italy.

I want to publicly thank Donato Sartori, master mask maker from Italy, for his gracious hospitality as I visited for one week in his workshop and studio. I have taken the liberty of illustrating the Title Page that precedes each major section of this book with photographs I took during this visit.

Donato has been most generous in his efforts to spread the technology of mask making.

CONTENTS

PREFACE

Students gather for an impromptu breakfast before they enter the studio for their mask-making workshop at the Centro Maschere e Strutture Gestuali, Albano Terme, Padova, Italy.

THE MATERIALS OF MASK MAKING

This book focuses on the practical side of mask making. The primary goal is to illustrate the techniques of crafting lightweight, comfortable character masks. A page or two, here and there, ponders some of the more elementary problems of mask design; the section on Commedia dell'Arte (page 101) discusses the interpretation of the traditional commedia characters; but for the most part we concentrate on the *crafts* of mask making. The text considers the advantages and disadvantages of a variety of available mask-making products. It examines the characteristics of each material and explains why you might choose one material for a particular mask instead of another.

There are about a dozen materials you can choose from to construct a successful mask.

sheet metal
fur
papier-mâché strips
glue cloth
latex
neoprene
Hexcelite (orthopaedic tape)
thermoplastic (Friendly Plastic)
vacuum-formed styrene
Celastic
leather

It might occur to you to ask, "Which material is best?" If there were a quick answer to this, we could concentrate on that single material. But there is no quick answer.

Expert mask makers do not agree. Some maskers make and perform exclusively in papier-mâché. Others, perfecting techniques of working with neoprene, prefer this medium. Many craftsmen and performers insist on leather. When it is left in its natural condition, each material has a texture that is uniquely its own.

Do not be led into false assumptions by the amount of space this book may take to explain a technique. Hammered metal and Friendly Plastic require more pages to demonstrate, but this does not recommend them as particularly superior materials. Papier-mâché and neoprene, which are easier to explain and thus receive less attention, may be better materials for general purpose masks. There is no single easy answer, so let's explore the possibilities of the various materials without prejudice.

MASK-MAKING CONSIDERATIONS

Consider the following points as you plan your mask and search for the appropriate medium for crafting it.

1. *A mask must be comfortable.* No doubt the most important consideration is that of comfort. If a performer is to wear the mask, it must fit! There are several ways to assure a proper fit. You will be certain of a perfect fit if you build the mask directly over a life mask of the performer.

The mask made from a flexible material nearly always fits, bending to conform to many face shapes. Latex rubber is the most flexible material that we will discuss here. A mask made of fabric or latex fits satisfactorily on almost every face without any additional effort on the part of the mask maker. Leather has excellent flexibility. Vacuum-formed styrene and papier-mâché masks are less flexible, but even these fit several faces if the bone structures are similar. Sheet metal, neoprene, Celastic, and thermoplastic materials are firm and unyielding. The most expedient way to fit a mask made of these materials is to custom adapt a slightly oversized mask. You simply fill the voids between the mask and the face with foam rubber or felt.

A mask must be lightweight. It must not shift with head movement. Vacuum-formed styrene is the lightest material that we will consider here, but papier-mâché, latex, and leather are also very lightweight. You must securely strap a large mask made of Celastic, metal, or neoprene to the performer's head because these materials are heavier.

The part of a mask touching the wearer's face must never have rough edges which could chafe with continued use. Vacuum-formed styrene is a winning choice here because the surface is very smooth. Neoprene and thermoplastic are also very smooth. Leather is very even textured, and although it is not the smoothest material, it has excellent comfort for other reasons. Papier-mâché, Celastic, and Hexcelite have rough, uneven surfaces. The interior of these masks require padding to make them comfortable.

2) *A mask must not physically interfere with the actor's ability to perform.* A performing mime or dancer can appropriately wear a full face mask. When the actor must speak, however, a half mask that leaves the mouth free is essential. And, while you are designing the jaw line, consider how to cut large holes in the nostrils so breathing is not impaired. A mask must never interfere with a performer's ability to speak, breathe, or see. Design and cut the eye holes large enough so the performer can see comfortably in all directions. And leave plenty of clearance in the eyelash area. When the actor blinks, the eyelashes cannot touch any part of the mask.

Choose an easily ventilated material for your mask. Sweat collecting between an actor's face and the material of his mask is intolerable. Leather is far and away the most absorbent material, "breathing" with the performer. A papier-mâché or Celastic mask backed with felt or foam rubber is sometimes absorbent and satisfactory, but no material can compare with leather.

3) *A mask must have the durability necessary for the sometimes rigorous ordeal of a long run.* Leather, Celastic, latex, foam latex, and neoprene are all very durable materials. Vacuum-formed styrene and papier-mâché are the big losers on this count.

4) *Is there any chance that the material you have chosen is going to be dangerous to use?* Happily, most of the materials of mask making are absolutely harmless. The hazardous chemicals of molding and casting do not lend themselves to mask making. The most risky materials demonstrated in this book are neoprene and Celastic, but even these are not considered threatening when you follow simple precautions.

5) *How economical is the mask-making medium?* Consider the costs of the materials and your time. There are considerable differences in the cost of the raw materials. At this writing, an undecorated papier-mâché mask costs about fifty

cents to make. A piece of leather to make the same mask could cost $10.00. That's twenty times more expensive. Still, if you are only making a few masks, the cost of the raw materials is probably not a major consideration.

Likewise, the ease of producing a mask varies a lot. Latex, neoprene, and vacuum-formed styrene are fast and effortless. If you have a mold ready, you can produce an undecorated mask with about twenty minutes of additional labor. Papier-mâché, Celastic, and glue cloth are easy enough, but they take as much as three or four hours construction time. Leather, without a doubt, takes the most time. A leather mask requires about five hours of attention, spread over a 24-hour period, to tool the shape. Then another five hours of care are needed to finish it.

MASKS AND PERSONA

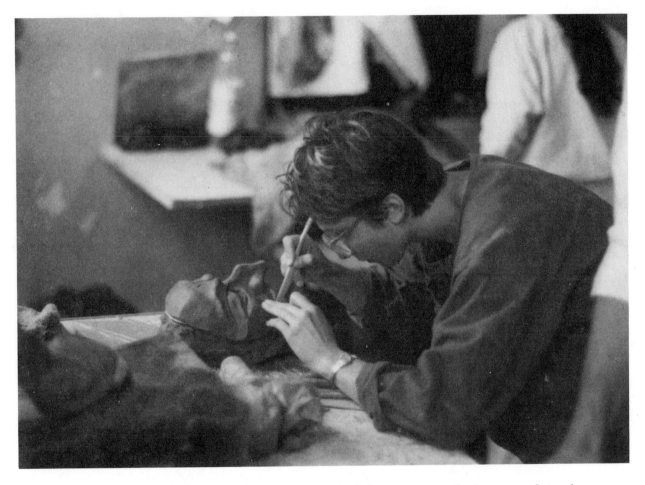

Rebecca Kravetz, a student of the summer workshop 1988, sculpting a mask in clay.

Mask

It may be helpful to point out to Americans that most peoples of the world disagree with us as to what a mask is. We think of it as a face covering, they (almost to a man) combine the elements that we call mask, costume, and the persona of the character into one single idea—that of "mask." The word "mask" makes many Americans think of a Halloween false face, or the eye covering of the Lone Ranger. In Europe, South America, Australia, and Africa, no strong verbal distinction is made between the face covering and the rest of the costume. The single word "mask" stands for a total disguise and more. It also includes all of the prescribed gestures, movement, and dance that are associated with the character being portrayed. The spirit of the character, person, or deity is frequently referred to as a mask.

Masque

The nearly antiquated word "masque" carries some of the idea of this unity. The masque of 17th century England used masks, but the term also includes the story and the style of presentation.

Maskers

Performers who use masks all agree that the mask has a spiritual life, a life which the ceremonial masqueraders of Africa believe is sacred, and which the performers of Japanese Nō dramas and commedia dell'arte consider to be secular, but just as vital. During the rehearsal period, it is not unusual for the spirit of the mask to lead the way. At these times the performer is a follower, learning the way, absorbing, preparing for the day when he will retrace the steps, this time as the leader, in full command.

In America, there is sometimes small sympathy for this concept. Here, a performer rehearses with his director for six weeks, and then, too often, meets his costume and mask at the first dress rehearsal. The mask, rather than being an aid, is a hindrance. The actor has two or three days at most to get over being bothered by his decoration.

Mask Makers

An ideal situation is for the performer to design and craft his own mask. This way the character and the mask are on the same course from the outset. The performer can refine the character's emotions as he sculpts the traits into the face. Then he can gain familiarity with his new persona as he builds the mask. The actor and his mask should be partners from the outset. He does well to invite his mask (the face covering) in as an active participant in the creation of the character. And the association should begin long before the first rehearsal.

If the performer is not a craftsman he may engage an artisan to construct his mask. The performer and his mask maker, however, must come to understand each other through lengthy discussions and many drawings. By the time the performer and his mask begin their first rehearsals they will already share many basic attitudes.

EARLY MAN
AND HIS MASKS

A mask being designed in a very fine water-based clay by Tina Tait.

ORIGINS

If we want to understand the origins of masks and why our ancient ancestors first used them, we must try to get an insight into the complex beliefs that motivated early man's actions. It will help if we can shed some of our civilized attitudes and openly acknowledge the omens that we read into everyday events. Let's recognize the taboos that influence us — the superstitions that we outwardly scoff at, then privately acknowledge as they prompt our actions.

Early man knew magic as an unexplained but functioning cause and effect relationship that he experienced on a very practical level. Although the practitioners of this art, past and present, may not be aware of it and do not want to analyze it, they put their trust in two basic principles of sympathetic magic.

1. *Like produces like, or, the belief that an effect has a literal resemblance to its cause.* The practitioner is confident that he can produce any circumstance he desires by imitating it.

The rainmaker beats a drum to induce thunder, and sprinkles water on the ground to draw rain from the sky.

A barren woman from the Babar Archipelago makes a wooden image of a child and holds it under her skirt. The native magician does several rude things with a live chicken, finally sacrificing it. When the ceremony is over, word goes out that the woman has conceived. Her friends come with congratulations. The pretense that a child has been born thus ensures that a child *will* be born.

On the eve of a hunt the men dress in the skins of their prey. Thus costumed, they play out an elaborate mime of the kill. They are confident that the drama will confirm their success.

2. *Things once in contact continue to act on each other after the contact has been severed.*

The most familiar example of contact magic is that of the voodoo doll. The belief holds that any severed portion of a man (his hair or nails) is in magical sympathy with his body. A doll made from these body parts can do harm or destroy the living body even from a great distance.

A mystic relationship is thought to exist between a wounded man and the weapon which made the wound. Roger Bacon, 13th century philosopher and alchemist, was aware of the theory and speaks on the subject. "It is constantly received and avouched," he writes, "that the anointing of the weapon that maketh the wound will cure the wound itself. I am not fully inclined to believe it." It seems, however, that he believes it a little, for he goes on to explain how to make the healing ointment from "the moss on the skull of a dead man unburied, and the fat from a bear killed in the act of regeneration."

When a Cingalese is dangerously ill, his relatives summon a local devil dancer. Dancing in appropriate costume and mask, he calls the demons of disease from the sick man's body and into his own. He feigns death. The relatives carry the devil dancer outside the village to the place for the dead. Being left to himself, he miraculously finds life again, and the sick man enjoys complete recovery.

The devil dancer, healer, rainmaker, or exorcist uses the most accurate device he knows of to portray his assumed character. He dons a mask, thus becoming the object of his imitative dramas. He also relies on the mask to hide his own identity as he officiates at the ritual.

The major masquerades of western civilization, Halloween, Mardi Gras, and the Venice carnival, were once tied to holy days and had important religious meaning. These celebrations have lost this meaning and are now a festive party commemorating forgotten events. Our society's use of the mask has become trivial compared to the serious and meaningful masquerades of our world neighbors.

The universality of these magical ceremonies is somewhat remarkable. You can find practices in the Congo, New Guinea, or Mexico very similar to those in the West Indies, Alaska, or the outback of Australia.

As recently as 200 years ago, the scene that follows might well have been played in any part of our globe. The performances are now rare, but you can still witness this scenario being enacted in some parts of the world today.

THE INITIATE

It was decided—I am to be the coyote.

The elders' council continued late into the night. Huddled in the middle of the group, nearest the fire, we were reminded again and again that we are no longer boys. "The time has come to leave your mothers," we were told. We are men and must learn to do the work of men: to hunt, to make weapons, to fight bravely, and to learn the ways of our totem ancestors.

Our village priest made his entrance, splendidly dressed in furs and bright feathers. His headdress was very large and contained great power. It was made from the skins of "all" animals. It was ornamented with the antlers and tails of the mild and quiet, and was jeweled with the claws and teeth of the great killers. He danced slowly, searchingly, attending to the leading of the spirits, while the elders droned a totem chant. The night passed. Through the magic of smoking, dancing, chanting, and scratching on the dirt floor, the path that each of us must follow was made clear to the elders. The youngest boy in our group will grow to be the bat. The oldest was declared brother of the jackal. It was revealed that my best friend is the elk, and I am to be the coyote. I am glad. The coyote is a clever fighter and hard to catch. The coyote is a trickster with strength in his great cunning. He is the wisest of all. I will work hard to be a good coyote.

Five days ago we were taken from the huts of the women to this secret spot in the forest. The place is known only to the men and the animals. The elders have worked in turn, counseling and teaching us the secret traditions of our tribe. We have earned knowledge of the tribe's secrets be-cause we have suffered; our newly selected totem will remain a secret of the men of our tribe; if our totem is killed or even harmed, we are also in great danger; and we must keep the secrets of the spirits from the women and our enemies.

Although it is summer, a hot burning campfire has been fed all the time. If our heads drop in weariness we are prodded to wakefulness. The old men have had much to tell us, lessons they have learned in their long life of studying and living with their own totems. But our village witch doctor has been our principal teacher. He teaches us to deposit our souls into the safekeeping of our totem animals and that in exchange we will receive magical powers. I have genuine respect for this wizard, but I am not afraid of him. I am deeply impressed, and awed, and I feel guilty that I am not frightened as the others are.

The magician is entering the ring of initiates again, his body covered with white clay. I see his mask is woven from long leaves. His forehead, elbows, waist, and knees are wreathed with thin, stringy bamboo leaves. His lesson is on the spirits of the plants and how to live with them.

My mind wanders, resting with fascination on the witch doctor's graceful movements and the strange tones as he imitates the voices of the spirits. I think: "I would like to be a holy man like this." I wonder if I could be his pupil. I could help him a lot, caring for the things of his priesthood; I could dig roots and gather the herbs he uses in healing and exorcisms. Studying to be like the coyote will be most useful. I will talk to him about this when we get home again. I am sure he will welcome my help.

EARLY MASK-MAKING MATERIALS

The masks on this page are contemporary creations by craftsmen of Mexico and Africa. Although the masks are not ancient, the materials are. Many of the techniques have changed very little from the days of antiquity.

This mask was made in Sonora, Mexico. It depicts the pharisee "Chapakobam" and has been used in Easter Week celebrations. It is a full head covering, made of goat skin stitched up the forehead and the back side.

Hair has been shaved from the cheek area, and some of the facial features have been applied with paint. The nose is a separate piece of hide sewn in place. Sheet metal plates make up the eyes; multiple holes have been drilled in the plate to allow the performer to see. Paper flowers decorate the forehead, ears, and back of the mask.

This anthropomorphic mask was made and used in Nigeria. It is carved from several pieces of wood which have been nailed together. The mask is rather large, measuring almost 36 inches tall, and heavy.

The masker gains two feet of height as he wears this mask, seeing through slits carved in the space beneath the nose.

This mask was also designed in Nigeria. It is worn there as part of a dance costume. The mask is carved from wood, and the hair is made of raffia grass. It too is about 36 inches tall, but it is much lighter.

(Photos by Richard Todd, courtesy of UCLA Museum of Cultural History)

Plant fibers and copper plates have been woven to make this face from Zaire. The hammered copper sheeting is attached to a framework made of carved wood. The hair is represented by basket-woven balls.

Animal Fur Masks

It is reasonable to assume that early man's very first venture into mask making began with animal skins. Our imagination allows us to see him as he dons the fur of a freshly killed fox, wolf, or beaver and cavorts for the amusement of his friends, prompted by his good humor rather than any serious attempt at imitative magic.

The rabbit fur mask demonstrated here is not very different from the headdress just described. It has some refinements — stitching, pleating, and the cutting of eye holes — but is perhaps not so very different.

Making a Rabbit Fur Mask

The rabbit fur you can obtain from your local leather-crafts store is likely to have been treated with mineral tannins — probably a chrome solution. When you soak this fur in water, it stretches a little, allowing you to shape it into or over a mold. The fluff of the fur is very forgiving, hiding the places where folds form. When the fur dries, it retains a limp resemblance to the shape of the mold.

If, however, it is wetted again, it loses its shape completely. To be a successful mask, the formed fur must be treated in some manner to ensure that the pattern shape is faithfully preserved. This mask makes use of needle and thread to preserve the required shape.

Wetting the Leather

Soak the fur in warm water for a few minutes. Squeeze it repeatedly to assure complete saturation, then wring the pelt to expel all of the excess water. Drape the piece over a head-shaped pattern. We have chosen to use a Styrofoam wig form in this demonstration.

This single pelt was large enough to cover the head from the chin, over the crown, and back down again to the base of the neck.

We were careful to arrange the pelt so the nap of the fur would lie close to the face if stroked downward. You may want to arrange things differently, but give it some thought.

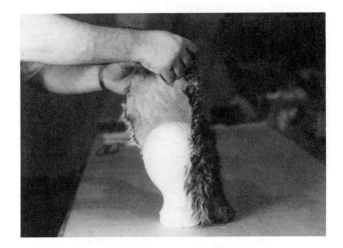

Stretching and Sewing the Fur

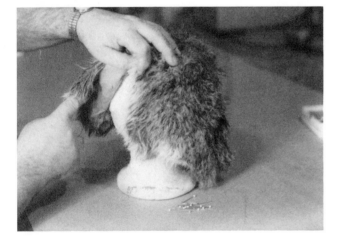

Stretch the wet fur around the form, putting some pressure on the nose. Use large headed dressmaker's pins to hold the skin centered and taut.

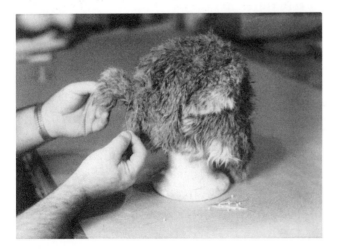

The fullness that falls naturally at the sides of the head makes a conspicuous suggestion of ears. Distribute the fullness to emphasize the appearance of ears, and pin the pleat.

Sew up the fur on both sides of the head. Remove the pins as you go.

Locating and Cutting the Eyes

Locate the position of the eyes. Using a new razor blade, shave a patch of fur from the eye area. Make the patch larger than the pupil of the eye — it will shield the eye from stray wisps of rabbit fuzz. It is also worth noting that the flying fuzz is easier to control if you do the shaving while the fur is still wet.

Cut a slit from the center of the shaved patch to make eye holes. Let the fur set overnight to dry.

It was mentioned earlier that unbacked rabbit fur tends to remain limp. You must make a tapered support if you want to hold the ears upright. We used a piece cut from the small end of a cardboard thread spool. Hot glue holds it in place.

Making Eyebrows

Cut eyebrows from a piece of scrap fur with a sharp razor blade. Each eyebrow will be about ¼ inch wide, and 1½ inches long at the skin. The fur, of course, flares out and makes the brow appear much wider.

 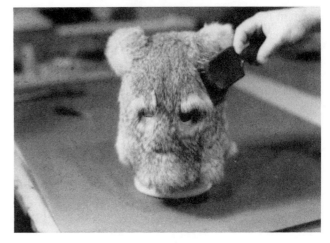

Locate the eyebrows in the lower portion of the forehead, comb the fur back, and hot glue the eyebrows in the depth of that part of the pelt.

Sew a pair of very small pleats below the nose to help define the nostrils.

Preserving the Shape with Varnish

Another way to assure that a piece of fur holds its shape after it is formed is to coat the interior with shellac or varnish. As the shellac dries, the skin becomes stiff and impervious to any further ef-

fects of water.

One further method of making a mask of animal fur is demonstrated in the section on Decorating Techniques (page 95).

Metal Masks

Hammering a relief pattern in the surface of metal is at least as old as Tutankhamen of Egypt; sculpted metal pieces using this technique were found in his tomb.

Evidently, early American Indians in the area of Mississippi also possessed the secrets to this craft. Several years ago we produced Lanford Wilson's *The Mound Builders*. The script calls

for a bronze ceremonial mask that has been excavated from a dig in Mississippi.

Since an authentic mask would be very precious, and it seemed reasonable that in this age of high technology, we should be able to do anything that a prehistoric Southerner could do, we built the mask to meet our need.

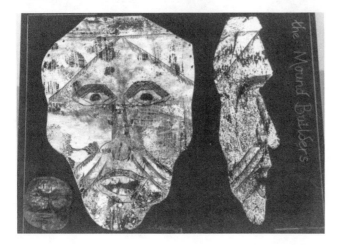

Elaine Ramiras designed this mask, working from a photo of an authentic mask of the Mississippian era. Rendered in gold foil and ink on black paper, it showed full face and profile views.

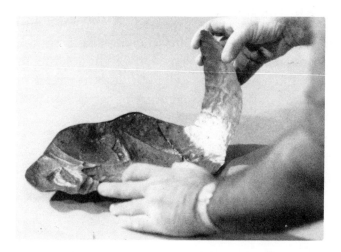 

When the sheet was shaped (according to the techniques demonstrated on the next page) it was fitted with a sort of skullcap. This allowed the witch doctor (or performer) to wear the mask in the execution of his business. We aged and textured the mask with black, brown, and green dyes to remove the bright luster and give a corroded look.

This mask (which was on display on the shelves in our prop room) was seen recently, and we were asked to build a set of similar metallic masks for a production of Andrew C. Ordover's new play, *The King of Infinite Space*.

Chasing and Repoussé

"Repoussé" and "chasing" are both terms for relief patterns hammered in sheet metal. Strictly speaking, repoussé refers to stamping or hammering a pattern from the reverse side. Chasing is done from the front of the figure to improve the details of the pattern. We will be using both of these techniques, but the bulk of the work will be done repoussé. You can shape most metals using this technique; of course, the soft metals are shaped more easily. We used copper, brass, and soft aluminum in building the set of fifteen masks for this production.

Building a Pitch Box

A pitch box is essential to the project. You fill the box with a soft, tough, shock-resistant material called "chasing pitch." This material acts as a cushion, receiving the blows of the hammer as the brass is formed. The cushion must be soft enough to change its shape when it is gently struck with a hammer, and tough enough to absorb the shock of these repeated blows. Roofing tar is frequently used as the cushioning material. Roofing tar is inexpensive, but not generally available in hardware stores. It must be purchased from a roofing supply yard.

When roofing tar is heated, it becomes thin, runny, and sticky, but when it again assumes room temperature, it has all the right qualities for the pitch box. Use an electric turkey roaster as an oven to raise the temperature of the tar to 180°F.

Build the chasing box of ¾ inch pine or plywood, with a Masonite backing. The box should be a little larger in both its width and length than the desired size of the mask.

We will use the box in the illustration to make half masks. It is designed to accept a brass, aluminum, or copper sheet sized at 6″ × 12″. We made another similar box for larger masks. It accommodated a sheet of metal 10″ × 12″.

The sides of the boxes are cut round so that when the metal plate is tacked in place it follows the general shape of a face even before the actual metal pounding begins.

Fill the box with its cushioning material to a level about ½ inch below the top edge of the curved bed.

It is difficult to make tar flow evenly into a box with curved side boards. You must fill it in stages. Fill one end, let it cool and solidify, then tip the box to the other end and fill it, etc. The tar pot must be returned to the oven between pourings to keep it hot and liquid.

Use a heat gun to melt the surface layers of tar. As the tar flows, the several pourings of tar blend together, losing their individuality.

Tooling the Sheet

Transfer your mask design to a sheet of metal with a black felt pen, and tack the sheet to the box.

Patiently and repeatedly strike the brass plate with the peen end of a hammer. Make the blows gentle and general at first. Keep stretching the soft metal plate till it finally rests on the cushioning material lying beneath it. Continue with gentle patient blows roughing the general shape into the sheet of metal. The deeper depressions of the profile do not receive more *powerful* blows, only more of them. Work gently, slowly, patiently.

As it touches the bed of tar, the metal sheet clings to the sticky surface. It is a combination of this adhesion and the shock absorption of the tar that protects the metal from tearing. Concentrate your hammer on the details of the mask's features. Carefully controlled blows of your hammer makes the mask conform to the design.

Chasing Tools

Make the smaller facial details by using blunt-end chasing tools. The punches shown here are specially made for tooling metal, but smooth-faced tools used for stamping designs in leather perform very well on soft metals and will show minimum signs of wear.

Use the chasing tool even more gently. Good detail is possible, as your tool directs the force onto a much more confined area. Slow and easy does it, and the sheet will not tear.

As soon as the sheet does tear, you must stop work in that area or the tear will grow.

When the mask is shaped to your satisfaction, remove it from the pitch box. If the sheet of metal clings to the tar bed and will not let go, simply heat the plate with the heat gun to melt it loose.

Melted tar can be scrubbed off the metal with turpentine or white gas.

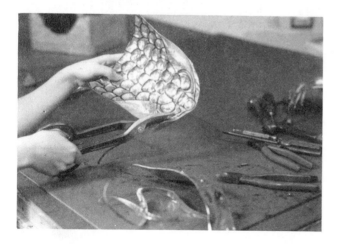

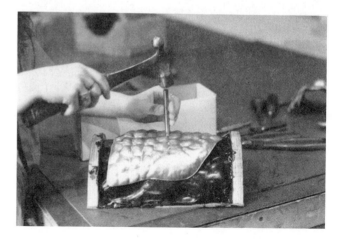

Trim the mask with a pair of tin snips. Follow the markings that you drew with the felt pen when the mask design was first transferred to the brass sheet.

Turn the mask over, onto a convex bed of cushioning tar. Work on the face of the relief pattern with chasing punches to improve the appearance of the features.

Cutting the Eyes

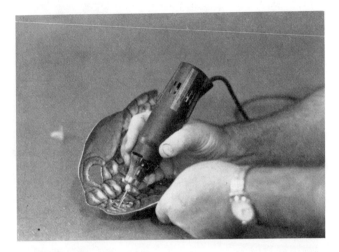

Drill several small holes into the eyes. Then use a small, hand-held grinder to file away all the remaining metal till the eyes are completely opened.

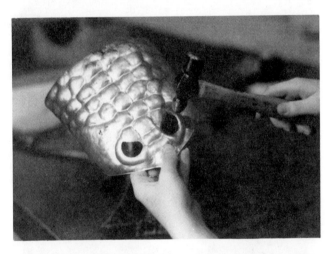

Put a rounded edge on the newly opened eyes. Rest the edge of the eye on the pointed end of an anvil and gently tap on the rim of the eye with a small ball-peen hammer. Continue the gentle tapping as you slide the eye of the mask along the anvil.

This mask took an evening to make. It is ready to be drilled and fitted with a headband.

These masks are in progress, and are in different stages of completion.

If you do not want the mask to be the bright color of new metal, you can treat it with dyes and spray paints.

The flame of a propane torch will heat-burnish brass or copper.

Sara Davis designed these masks and is shown here applying color and tarnish to the completed faces.

LIFE MASKS

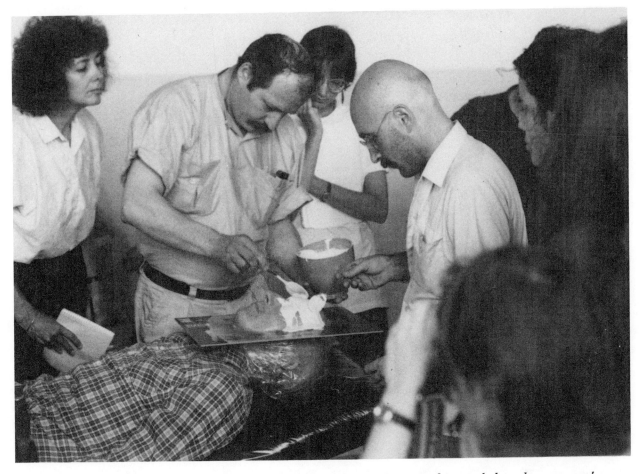

Master mask maker Donato Sartori instructing the students in his workshop how to make a life mask in plaster. The model is Professor Tom Wheatly.

Egyptian priests made clay facsimiles of their kings when they died, to decorate their tombs and to perpetuate their existence. These copies taken from the dead were called "death masks." It didn't take long for the priests to improve their techniques so these masks could be taken from the faces of living kings, thus producing "life masks." All they had to do was provide a way for their subject to breathe during the sitting. This was accomplished by leaving an unfinished flaw in the tip of the nose, and subsequently finishing it, modeling it by hand, or by having the model breathe through straws which reached through the casting material. The techniques have remained unchanged these several thousand years.

Uses for Life Masks

Life masks have proven very helpful when applied to the needs of the theater. Makeup artists can build appliances (reshaped noses, chins, eyebrows, etc.) that fit the actor perfectly because such an appliance can be sculpted over a direct replica of the performer. You can assure a perfect fit, when making any character mask, if the performer's life mask is used as the basis for sculpting his new character's face. The life mask is also an ideal base from which to begin sculpting a neutral mask.

For many hundreds of years life masks have been made from plaster. This traditional material can still be used, but alginate is recommended today, because it does a better job and is safer.

Alginate

Alginate (pronounced with a soft "g") is a gelatin made from seaweed. It is the same material that dentists use (flavored strawberry) for making dental impressions. There are not many other molding materials that are completely harmless to the human body. Alginate is organic, non-toxic, non-drying, and in every way inoffensive to our physical machinery. This material that will not harm the tender membranes on the inside of your mouth will certainly do no damage to your model's suntanned, wind worn, calloused hide. Alginate is flexible, very fast setting, gives high resolution, and will not adhere to anything unless it is embedded in it—not even to itself.

MAKING A LIFE MASK FROM ALGINATE

The subject who is having his face copied must be willing. A model with tendencies toward claustrophobia may have a real mental struggle about submitting to the ordeal. Sometimes someone can be enticed into cooperating with the promise of a copy of his face for his very own to take home. Vanity can overcome fear.

Make your model as comfortable as possible. Put a pillow under his head and lay him flat on his back.

When the alginate is applied over his face, all of his breathing will be done through soda straws (the larger size, such as those that come with a milk shake). At this point have the model fit

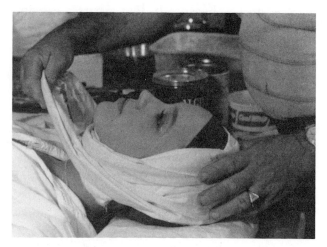

straws into his nostrils to see how it feels, and to be assured that breathing will indeed be possible and comfortable. As soon as our model has a measure of confidence, the straws can be removed till later.

The model's face should be washed thoroughly: a man should be well shaven; a woman must remove all her makeup.

Although a release agent is not absolutely necessary when working with alginate, a light coat of petroleum jelly on the eyelashes and eyebrows makes them lie close to the skin's surface, and keeps the pattern of crossed hairs from getting embedded in the hardened alginate.

Protect your subject's hair with a tight fitting shower cap or a nylon stocking.

Swathe your model's head with a piece of muslin, loosely wrapping it around, from chin to crown. This helps control the alginate, keeping it on the facial features while it is in a liquid, runny form (and keeping it out of the model's ears).

Cured alginate is very flexible. It is therefore necessary to back it up with rigid reinforcement

made of cheesecloth and plaster. The plaster reinforcement is called a "mother mold."

So, while the model is preparing and before you mix the alginate, cut three pieces of cheesecloth 12″ x 24″, and mix up about a quart of plaster to make this reinforcement. Look ahead to the section on Mixing and Using Plaster (page 57) for detailed directions on how to mix plaster.

It takes mixed plaster about 20 minutes to begin to get firm, so it will be just about ready to use when you are finished with the alginate, if you have the materials prepared and proceed with confidence. Add the plaster to the water as suggested in the text but do not stir the ingredients. You will do the actual stirring after the alginate has set up solidly.

Alginate comes in powder form. It should be mixed with water and used *immediately*. It must be thoroughly mixed in one minute, and then poured directly onto the desired casting pattern (the face). In three minutes it will have set up and be ready for removal. Now, that's not much time for false moves. If you mix the powder with very cold water, you will have more time. (Ice water more than doubles the work time, but ice water gets uncomfortable.) Anyhow, you won't need more time; just be ready to act, and proceed with confidence.

The alginate mix comes with a scoop for measuring the powder and a small vial for measuring the correct amount of water. One measure of each is presumed to be ample for making a dental impression; however, to make a life mask, you will need 25 times this amount. Measure out 25 scoops of powder into one mixing bowl and 25 vials of water into another. (When you have gained experience with this product, you may not want to continue measuring the components. You will estimate the amount of powder and stir in water till the consistency seems right. But that's for later.)

Pour the powder into the bowl with the water, and your three minute countdown begins. Put all of your attention to the task of mixing these ingredients. You may use an electric cake mixer or an electric drill fitted with a paint stirring paddle, or you may stir with a spatula and concentrated energy. Mix the paste as if you were mixing up a cake; in fact, the mixed alginate will look almost like cake batter.

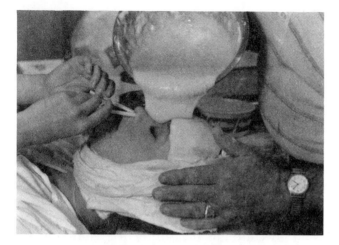

Tell your subject to place the straws in his nostrils. (When he sticks the straws in himself, it is much less likely to tickle the nose hairs.) After one minute of mixing, pour the alginate onto your subject's face.

From this point on, the subject must keep his eyes closed. At this stage, therefore, you should begin a narrative of everything you are doing, so as to keep him informed, comfortable, and confident as to what is happening in his surroundings. Use your most soothing bedside manner.

As you begin to spread the alginate, advise the subject that you are beginning to apply the mixture to his right cheek and that it will be cold. Warn him not to flex his facial muscles, and assure him that if he feels panic at any time he can abort the process by simply sitting up. All you will have lost will be a few minutes time and a little alginate.

If the process is being observed, all joking on the spectators' part must now cease. Any uncontrolled facial movement will ruin the cast.

Soon, the alginate will be set up to the consistency of very firm gelatin. It must now be reinforced with the plaster mother mold spoken of earlier. Without it the alginate can flex out of shape, and the features will distort unrecognizably. Ask your subject to begin patiently flexing his facial muscles in an effort to loosen the gelled casting from his skin. This will give him a diversion while you are making the mother mold.

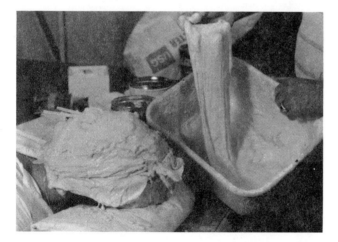

Fetch your tub of soaking plaster. It should have been no more than 7 or 8 minutes since you introduced the water, and it is now ripe for use. Give the mixture its first stirring, and it will become fluid. Dip in the prepared pieces of cheesecloth, saturating them thoroughly in the plaster.

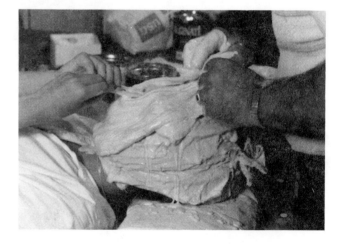

Drape the plaster-cloths one at a time around the alginate mold. Press and work the plaster-saturated gauze onto the form of the alginate. The plaster will not stick to the alginate, rather it conforms to the precise shape offered by the mold, making a hard shell support for the alginate.

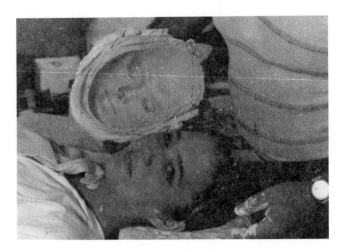

When the plaster has solidified, you may free your model from his confinement. Loosen the forehead first and then carry the mold down toward the chin. This will slide the straws out of the subject's nostrils.

MOLDING AND CASTING

We have already defined one important term: "mother mold." There are just a few more that you should know to help you understand the text to come.

Almost every mask you construct will be produced using a technique of molding and casting. The terms "molding" and "casting" can easily be confused. We can clear up this semantic problem, however, with one sentence of explanation. *A mold is the pattern from which a casting is taken.* This single sentence defines both words.

It is not at all unusual for a casting to be used as a mold (from which subsequent castings can be made).

In mask making, the pattern (usually that of a sculpted form of clay, in the previous case a model's face) acts as a mold when it is covered with plaster. This plaster reproduction is called a casting until the moment it is pressed into service to make copies of its shape. Then it will correctly be referred to as a mold.

Positive and Negative Molds

A clay sculpture is considered to be a "positive" shape; the protruding features project forward, and the sunken features recede into the mold. A plaster casting taken from this form is called a

"negative" shape; the eye sockets lie nearest to you as you view the casting, and the nose and chin appear as the deepest hollows in the form. The alginate casting is negative.

Mold Release

The use of a mold release (an agent to ensure the casting doesn't stick to the mold) is normal in any casting procedure. It is a fact that alginate

will not stick to skin, and you will find that plaster will not stick to Plasticine, but a thin coating of a release agent can only be helpful.

Making a Positive Plaster Copy of the Life Mask

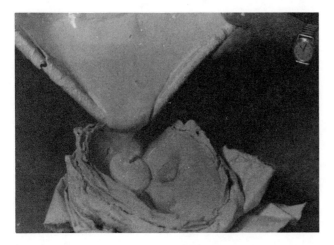

Make a positive copy of your subject's face by mixing a fresh batch of plaster and pouring it into the supported alginate. The alginate is now acting as a negative mold.

This copy can (and should) be made immediately. An alginate mold will shrink as the moisture dries out of it. This shrinkage is not a big problem for our purposes, but a dentist is cautioned to make his casting within the hour, or it will not fit his patient's mouth.

A plaster life mask such as this one can be used as the basis for making masks with the unique face shape of the model from whom it was taken.

It is a simple matter to separate the plaster casting from the alginate mold. The mold is still flexible and non-sticking. Just press the two apart, and take a look at your finished life mask.

THE NEUTRAL MASK

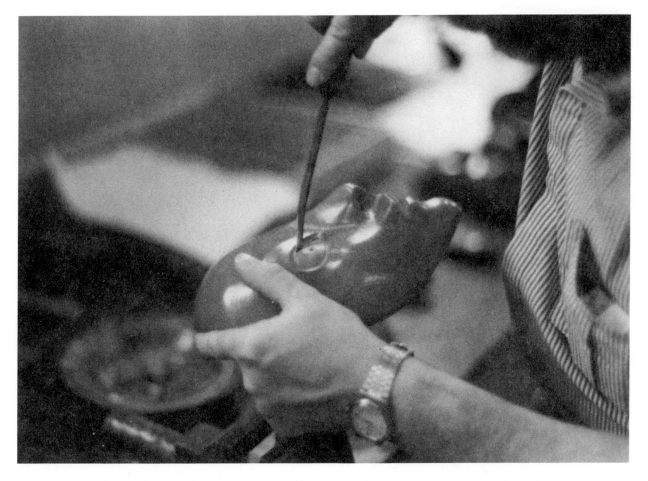

One of Sartori's craftsmen cutting open the eyes of this neutral mask.

The citizens of this world (you and I) are aware in a very practical way of the advantages of working with masks. Sunglasses, hair styles, beards, face jewelry, hats, and smoking accoutrements (pipe, cigar, cigarette) are types of veils we find useful to hide our shyness and insecurity. It is peculiar that when one's face is screened, there is a presumption that the whole person is somehow protected.

We feel safe behind our carefully chosen disguises, and are encouraged to assume the role the mask may suggest. We can now act "cool," "tough," "carefree," "fearless," "worldly," "mature," "sophisticated," etc. Like the ostrich with his head in the sand, we operate on the principle that if our face is hidden (or even partly so) our entire personality is secure. The ploy works for the ostrich, and it seems to work rather well for us.

The beginning actor experiences this same phenomenon as he makes his first explorations with a neutral mask. In these initial classroom exercises, the mask becomes a tool for depersonalization, reducing his inhibitions. Upon donning the neutral mask, it is common for an actor to experience his environment as though he had never seen it before. He assumes a baby-like perspective, seemingly discovering his surroundings anew, without feeling obliged to make judgments.

When an actor wears a half mask like the ones pictured here, his body is freed. He is encouraged to experiment. If his self-consciousness is overcome, in nearly every case the actor is able to go beyond his usual limits.

During these exercises, the performer sometimes learns to find and isolate the role that "self" plays in the process of character development. He is encouraged to use this awareness to enrich the character or, as is just as likely, once identified he may choose to reduce the effects of his obtruding ego.

In later exercises the neutral mask separates facial expression from body expression, forcing the body to carry a share of the load in conveying emotion. The full face mask silences the actor's two most powerful means of communication, his voice and his facial expression.

Karen Torell designed these neutral mask forms, male and female, sculpting them in modeling clay over plaster life masks. If a performer wants to relay an emotion while wearing this mask, he *must* use his body as the means of expression. It is absolutely futile to frown, smile, or scowl behind the mask — nothing is communicated.

DESIGNING A NEUTRAL MASK

Amleto Sartori, who made the masks for Jacques Lecoq's experiments with mime, strove to make the mask absolutely neutral—totally without expression. He began by making a casting of the actor's relaxed face and then, modifying it, he eliminated residual traces of expression. He concentrated on removing all of the details, no matter how small, that he felt would deprive the mask of its neutrality.

As Lecoq's experiments with mime progressed, he and Sartori decided that no single mask would work satisfactorily for both genders and that the neutral mask should be formatted in two styles, male and female.

In the book, *Behind the Mask,* Bari Rolfe refers to an expressionless mask as being a universal mask. The universal mask is not neutral but contains those traits that we all have in common. The design does contain the essential features of expression, but in the most economical way. The mask is not, therefore, devoid of emotion, but rather is capable of portraying many emotions.

Mime classes have been designed around the use of four basic age masks. Still retaining their neutrality of expression, these masks represent the four ages of man: adolescence, adulthood, mature age, and old age. Some examples of age masks will be found in the next section on Character Masks (page 53).

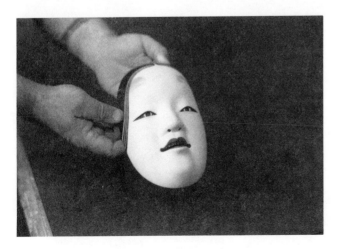

The class pictured here is investigating the art of acting with the use of a full face neutral mask made of leather. They are experimenting with methods of communicating through the use of posture and body movements.

The Japanese Nō theater uses full face masks in the performance of their dramas. Many of the masks designed for the young women, Ko-Omote, Waka-Onna, Zo-Onna, and others, appear to be neutral—lacking in expression. Although no obvious emotion is immediately projected, Ko-Omote can express a variety of feelings during a single performance with her physical manner. To cite one obvious example of this technique, the performer may depict sorrow by bowing her head, and project joy as the head is lifted. Remarkably, the mask seems to change its expression as the performer's pose is altered.

Sculpting a Mask with "Life"

Expert mask makers agree that a mask must have a life of its own. It is possible (and the occurrence rate is not low) to sculpt a mask that is *dead!* A dead mask will prove to be unsatisfactory in performance. A finished mask must contain a vitality that is contagious to the actor. The features carved into the mask should contain an energy not yet released but unmistakably there; a latent power that can draw from the actor an energy level slightly higher than that of ordinary life. This quality is difficult to define, but easy enough to detect in performance.

If you are looking for it, a dead mask can usually be detected and corrected in the clay stage as you are sculpting it. When you suspect that a mask is lacking the necessary vitality, you can prove it by making a quick copy of it in papier-mâché. Perform with it (or have someone else perform with it) to see if it can communicate.

CHARACTER MASKS

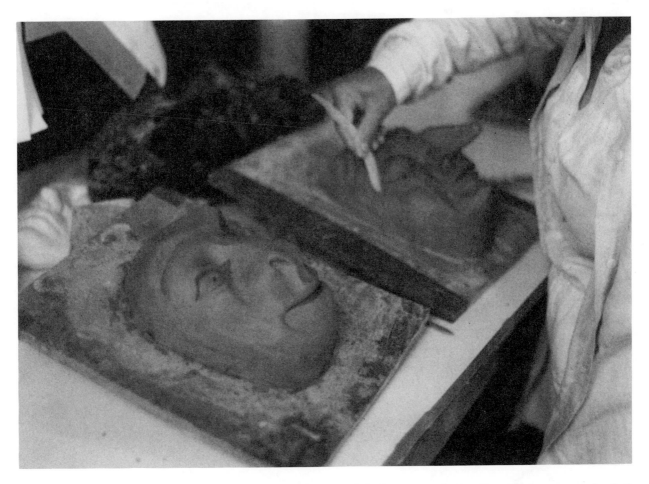

A workshop student, Yenudith Greenspan, has modeled two masks in clay. The one on the left was intentionally sculpted to contain some of the mule-like features of the campus mascot.

There has been a resurgence in the use of masks in the theater in recent years. In the last four years the production program at UCLA has used masks in at least twelve shows. Masks have played an incidental part in *The Mound Builders, Romeo and Juliet, Much Ado About Nothing, Macbeth, The Changeling,* and *The Boys from Syracuse.* Masks played a major role in our productions of *Medea, The Visit, Bottoms Up* (an original commedia dell'arte piece), *Takara No Tsuruhashi, The Dispossessed,* and *The King of Infinite Space.* The acting classes are using neutral masks in exercises. Students are also showing a keen interest in crafting masks just for fun, to wear at masquerades and celebrations such as The Renaissance Pleasure Faire and The Festival of Masks. In our theater productions we have, without exception, followed the traditional pattern of the costumer designing the masks as an integral part of the character's costume, and the property shop building the mask.

We have used the full range of products in preparing the masks, but no matter which material you choose, the steps you follow are almost always the same.

1. Design the mask, sketching the features on paper.

2. Sculpt the mask from clay, following the designer's drawings.

3. Make a negative plaster casting of the clay sculpture.

4. Make a positive hard mortar casting from the negative plaster form. (If your chosen material can be worked in a negative mold, skip this step.)

5. Craft the mask form from the material of your choice.

6. Fit the mask and add straps for attachment.

7. Paint and decorate the mask.

These steps are demonstrated and explained in detail on the following pages.

MAKING A NEGATIVE MOLD

Sculpting the Mask

Design your neutral mask in modeling clay. The clay can be either oil- or water-based. If you sculpt over a life mask, the proportions of the face are conveniently laid out for you. *The mass of the face is also defined.* A beginning sculptor almost always makes the features of his mask on a two dimensional plane, forgetting that a head has depth!

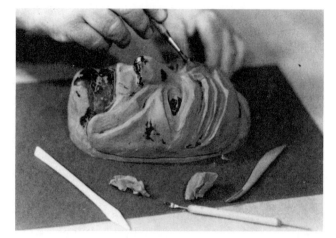

Applying Mold Release

Choose a release agent. Either green soap or petroleum jelly assures an easy release from plaster. Give the form a careful coating, making sure no part of the surface is skipped. Use a brush, cotton swab, wad of tissue, or your fingers to apply the coating. Keep this coating very thin. The casting will pick up the texture of the surplus release agent if a thick coating is applied, rather than the intended texture of the model.

Surround the pattern with a clay wall, about ¾ inch from the mask, and an inch or so tall. The use of a clay wall is a technique that controls the plaster when it is applied and assures that the casting does not get too thick. Apply some of the release agent to the clay wall and the base it lies on.

Mixing and Using Plaster

Plaster of Paris or casting plaster is as important to the art of molding and casting today as it was hundreds of years ago when it was first intro-

duced. Detailed directions on mixing this product are given here, but every time plaster is called for the mixing procedure will be the same.

A negative mask this size will require about three quarts of mixed liquid plaster. Begin with about two and a half quarts of water.

The manufacturers of plaster recommend that you mix plaster in a ratio of 7 parts water to 10 parts of the dry powder by weight. The following instructions for mixing plaster will give you approximately correct proportions without using a scale.

Sift dry plaster of Paris into the water. Do not stir the mixture. Keep adding plaster till the water is completely absorbed and will accept no more powder. The powder will increase the volume of the mixture to about three quarts.

The unstirred mixture will have the appearance of damp plaster powder—no islands of dry plaster anywhere, and not many little ponds of liquid either. Let the water and plaster steep for about 5 minutes, intermingling and getting acquainted. Now stir. Thorough mixing of the plaster is very important to the success of the final product. Undermixed plaster is not strong. You can use your hands to mix a small batch like this but you must stir for several minutes, till the mixture is uniform, with no lumps.

The mixture should be pourable, about the consistency of pancake batter, but we will not pour it. The retaining wall we built is too shallow to restrict the flow of plaster as thin as this. More

control is required, so you must ladle it onto the form slowly, patiently, constantly attending the process as the plaster begins to thicken.

Applying an Impression Coating

Carefully apply an impression coating of the liquid plaster to the entire surface of the pattern. Use a brush, or your fingers, making certain that no air is remaining trapped between the plaster and the surface of the sculpture.

Pouring the Mold

Apply more of the plaster mixture directly over the impression coating. Keep adding the plaster by handfuls until the flow of plaster begins to creep over the clay retaining wall. Wait patiently till the plaster gets firmer. If you use casting plaster (plaster of Paris) and the water is at comfortable room temperature, the whole process should take about 20 minutes.

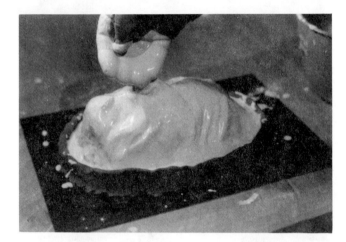

Monitor the progress of the thickening, and add more plaster as you are able. The firmer mixture will flow more and more sluggishly till finally the plaster will behave, staying where you put it. Make sure the whole form is covered to a nearly uniform depth of ¾ inch. The sides will tend to become too thick, and the area around the nose will tend to be too thin. So scoop some of the plaster off the sides and pile it back on the nose as gravity fights your efforts.

Soon, in about 20 minutes, the plaster will become so firm that it is no longer workable. Put a flat spot, a sort of mesa, on the top of the mold. This flattened area will allow the casting to remain steady when it is turned over for use later.

Wait for the plaster to harden. Plaster gets hot as it cures. Monitor the casting with your hands, feeling for this warmth.

Within an hour (depending on the casting's thickness and total volume) the casting will attain maximum temperature and begin to cool. Before it cools off completely, separate the Plasticine pattern from the casting.

If you used an oil-based modeling clay, it will be warmed by the curing plaster casting and become soft. The casting is easier to remove in this state, especially if there are minor undercuts in the mask. The casting will not achieve maximum

strength for several more hours, but it is still a good idea to make the separation while the modeling clay is warm and soft. Sometimes (as shown in the photo) the clay sculpture survives with a minimum of damage. Sometimes it is totally destroyed in the removal.

If you must build your mold over a positive pattern, this negative mold can be used to reproduce your mask design in a hard positive form. The process is demonstrated in the section on Making a Positive Gypsum Cement Mold (page 79).

CASTING A MASK IN A NEGATIVE MOLD

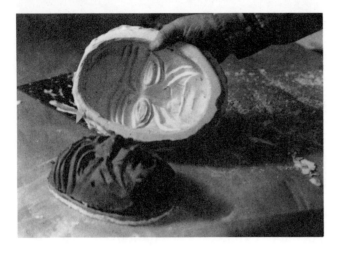

This plaster casting is ready to be used as a negative mold to make a mask. The next pages will show how negative mask forms can be used with several popular mask-making materials: papier-mâché, latex, neoprene, and a thermoplastic product called "Friendly Plastic."

Papier-mâché

Papier-mâché is another material that dates from antiquity. The masks used in classic Greek dramas were built up from pulped bark bound together with glue. Before this, witch doctors were making masks and headdresses of interlaced leaves and bark strips cemented into place with a form of wheat paste. Although the techniques are old, they have survived and are still usable.

There are several properties of papier-mâché that recommend it as a mask-making material. 1) It is lightweight. 2) It is inexpensive. 3) It is easy to work. 4) When backed with felt or thin strips of foam rubber it can be very comfortable. The big drawback to papier-mâché is that it is not durable and will not stand up to continued use or rough treatment.

Papier-mâché works best when you work the glue-soaked paper strips into a negative mold.

Applying Mold Release
The negative plaster mold must be prepared by giving it a light coating of petroleum jelly to act as a mold release. Cured papier-mâché will adhere to untreated plaster. It even does a pretty good job of clinging to the harder grades of oil-based modeling clay.

Another good aid to easy release, although not illustrated here, is to carefully apply one coat of wet paper (with no glue) over the entire greased pattern.

Preparing the Materials

There are several paper products with qualities that make them appropriate for papier-mâché work, and a few products without such qualities. Newspaper is excellent; brown wrapping paper (such as is used in making a grocery bag) works well and is stronger than newspaper. Paper toweling can be used; and tissue paper is recommended for the final coating if you want the smoothest surface.

The papers that do not work well have a hard or oily finish. Magazines are processed to resist moisture and water penetration, so the glue cannot soak into the fibers.

The glue you select for papier-mâché work should dry to form a hard shell-like surface. Brown carpenter's glue made from animal gelatine (the kind that has to be cooked) has traditionally been used in the theater for scenic papier-mâché work. It is still a good glue—it has excellent strength, and it sets up hard, making a rigid mask. Wallpaper paste and white (polyvinyl alcohol or PVA) glue cure to a softer finish, but are recommended because they are so much more convenient.

Applying the Paper Strips

Lay the pieces of glue-soaked paper, overlapping the edges, in a crisscross kind of patchwork. Apply the paper with your fingers, smoothing it down, blending the edges, and spreading out the excess glue. Use smaller pieces in areas of finer detail. Make extra tears around prominent features (such as the nose) to assure that the paper can lie flat without any hard fold lines. Continue this process till the entire mold is filled with glued strips.

After this first application, the mask may be as much as three layers deep, due to the overlapping.

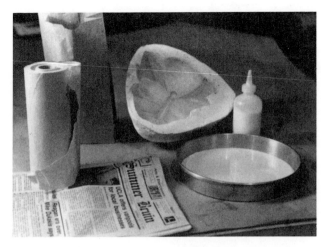

Prepare the paper by tearing it into strips about 1" × 3". Tear rather than cut the paper into pieces to eliminate any hard, clean cut, sharp edges. A torn strip has a slight taper in its edge which helps it to blend into the adjoining pieces. A scissored edge cannot blend well into the neighboring piece.

Dip several paper strips in glue and let them sit and soak. After they are saturated with glue, run the strips through your crossed fingers to remove some of the surplus paste, and lay them one by one into the negative mask form.

Applying the Second Coat

Lay a second coat of glue-soaked strips directly over the first application, using the same technique of application.

These strips should be prepared from a paper stock that has a different pattern or color. The color change works as a visual aid to help you know when the coating is complete and that there are no voids. Now, your casting should be six or eight layers thick. If you have been using newspaper, you could use the comic pages for the second coating. The illustration shows the second coating being made from torn pieces of a paper grocery bag.

Removing the Papier-mâché Casting

Allow a 48-hour drying period. The mask should be dry, firm, and strong. If not, set it aside till it is. Try to separate the mask from its mold. As the casting dries it shrinks slightly, allowing it to pull away from the sides of the negative mold.

Trimming the Mask

Trim the outline of the mask with a pair of scissors and open the eyes with a mat knife.

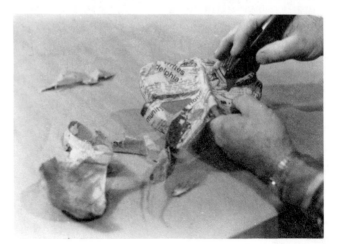

Applying the Finish Coat

Apply one final coat, right over the face of the mask. We have chosen to make this final coating from strong paper toweling.

The final coat bridges over the rough joints created by the heavier paper and makes a flaw-free surface, even when subjected to close inspection. Choose a paper that is thin but strong. Do not select a paper that is apt to dissolve or disintegrate when it is soaked in glue.

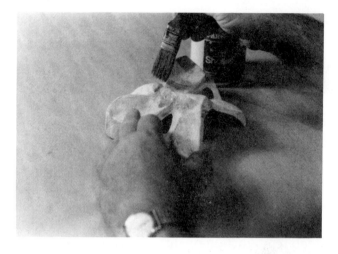

Seal the final coat with a coating of shellac. It is ready for paint.

If you want a smoother texture, it can be achieved by treating the mask with a lacquer primer. Allow the paint to dry and sand away the roughness. Repeated coatings and sandings will make the surface as slick as you want it.

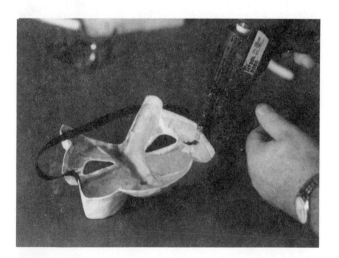

Add a strap to your mask by hot gluing elastic to the temples.

You can get unique surface textures by selecting different papers to use for the final covering. This mask has a very interesting texture because the final veneer was made of kraft paper.

Liquid Latex Rubber

Latex is the milky secretion of certain plants. There are a few other things added—a stabilizer, a preservative, and a solvent—but it's mostly those milky juices. On contact with the air, liquid latex coagulates and cures to a permanent flexible sheet of rubber.

Latex rubber can be cast into a very durable and at the same time very flexible mask. It is one of the most economical materials you could choose for mask making in terms of both labor and cost. Latex is lightweight and could be very comfortable but, due to its extreme flexibility, a latex mask can lie close to the performer's face, allowing pools of perspiration to collect. The finished mask can be helped, however, by cushioning it with absorbent cloth.

Preparing the Mold

Latex rubber forms best in a negative plaster mold. Prepare the mold, if necessary, by filling imperfections left by air bubbles with a small batch of spackling paste made of plaster. Then sand away any surface roughness. Latex has rather high reproduction qualities, picking up the form and features of a mold and also the details and flaws of its surface. A pit in the negative mold would show up as a wart on the face of the mask.

No mold release is necessary; a latex casting will easily part from many mold-making materials including plaster.

Pouring the Mold

Pour liquid latex into the prepared mold. It is not necessary to fill the mold completely. Just pour in enough of the liquid rubber so that, as you rotate the mold, tipping it from side to side, all surfaces of the mold are covered.

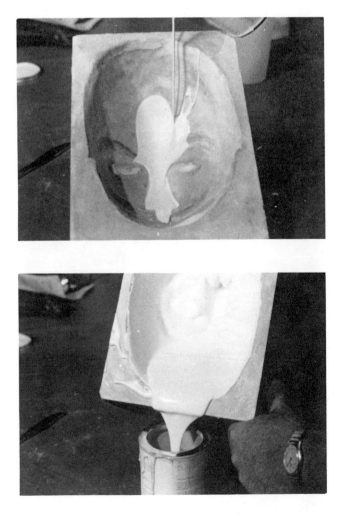

When the entire surface of the mold is covered, pour the excess latex back into the can. It is not contaminated and can be reused.

Curing the Latex

The curing of latex is a simple drying process, setting up as the solvent evaporates from the liquid. The open pores of the plaster also absorb solvent, assisting in the drying. It is possible to speed the process by force drying the latex with a hair dryer.

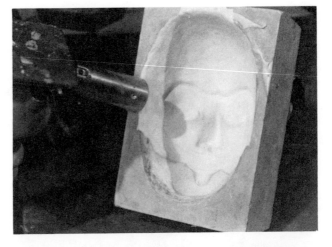

Laminating Cheesecloth

When the mask has cured, it can be made much stronger by implanting a layer or two of cheesecloth in the freshly dried first coating. Use more liquid latex as a bonding agent. Brush fresh latex into the open weave, embedding the fabric in the interior of the mask.

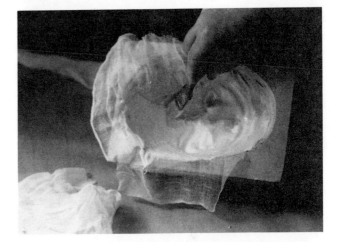

Attaching a Headband

Secure a head strap or elastic band to the temples of the mask by embedding it into the latex. Sew a cross of fabric to the strap, giving it a wide base for a firm attachment. Coat both surfaces with a fresh coat of latex. Press the wetted surfaces together and coat the top of the strap again, completely saturating the fabric and making it one with the latex of the mask.

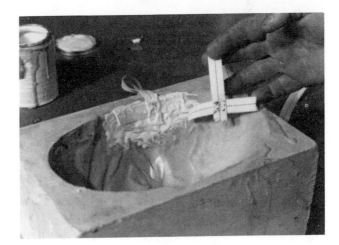

Opening the Mold

When the latex rubber is dry, pull it from the plaster mold. Latex separates from untreated plaster easily, so all you need to do is gently tug the mask, working in all directions from the cheeks, chin, and forehead inward to the nose area, to free it. The strong, flexible latex will pull away cleanly, even from all but the most serious of undercuts.

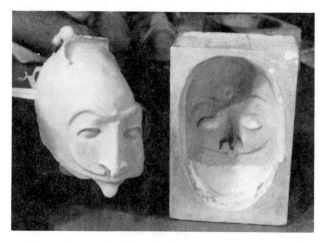

Trimming the Mask

Open the eyes and nostrils with a razor knife or fingernail scissors. Cut the mask to size and shape, and it is ready for paint and decoration.

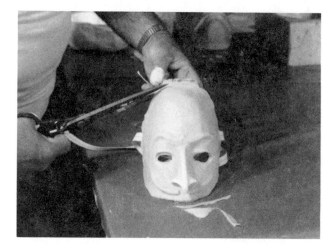

Painting a Latex Mask

Latex rubber is so flexible it must be painted with a coloring material that is equally flexible. Or, the paint must be extremely thin, to keep it from cracking and peeling from the rubber surface.

You can custom mix a paint, based in rubber cement, that works very well on latex. "Universal tinting colors" can be blended into the cement, producing any desired color. The blend can be thinned with naptha to good brushing consistency, or it can even be thinned enough to be sprayed. Latex can be painted with an airbrush, using either this homemade rubberized paint or dyes.

Neoprene Casting Rubber

Neoprene rubber is a formulation that was designed many years ago as a substitute for latex rubber. Neoprene casting rubber works a lot like the latex it was supposed to replace, but its characteristics are not the same. Some of these differences work to great advantage in mask making. The manufacturer of this product primarily caters to those who make Halloween and masquerade masks.

To make a neoprene casting, you use the age old pottery-making process of absorption casting. In this process you pour liquid neoprene into a plaster mold, and allow it to sit for a period. The plaster mold absorbs solvent from the neoprene just as the water is blotted from the clay in slip casting pottery. A thin wall forms, which remains clinging to the plaster mold when the bulk of the liquid is poured out. This thin wall becomes a strong casting as the neoprene cures through the joint efforts of evaporation and additional absorption.

Neoprene castings are very tough and durable. Neoprene is an easy medium to work with. You will certainly appreciate the ease when you must make a lot of copies from the same mask mold. The convenience of the technique must, however, be weighed against the nuisance of the necessary wait periods between pourings. Although neoprene is supposed to be a rubber product, it is not particularly flexible, especially when the walls become more than 1/8 inch thick. Thick-walled castings can also become heavy and cumbersome.

Preparing the Model

Sculpt the desired model from modeling clay. This mask, designed on a gnome motif, was sculpted over a life mask. You must use a positive clay sculpture such as this to make a negative plaster mold.

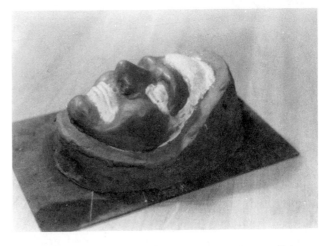

If you are sculpting in water-based modeling clay, use a drop or two of water to polish out rough spots left by your sculpting tools. If you are using oil-based modeling clay, use a drop of liquid soap or a little alcohol as a lubricant for smoothing the surface. If you use soap, use it very sparingly, being careful not to contaminate the surface. Apply a drop of soap to the clay and then use a little water on your finger to extend this drop over a large area, lubricating the surface as you polish it. Soap can also be used as a release agent to keep the plaster casting from sticking to the plaster parts of the model. A thin coat is sufficient, but don't skip any of the places where the plaster is exposed. *Do not use petroleum jelly as a mold release when you plan to make the final casting of neoprene.* It clogs the plaster and greatly contributes to failures in the final product.

Making the Plaster Mold

Mix up a batch of #1 pottery plaster. #1 pottery plaster is designed especially to be used in slip casting pottery and is very porous and absorbent. See the section on Mixing and Using Plaster (page 57) for detailed mixing instructions. Use the freshly mixed plaster while it is at its runniest to make an impression coating. Work the plaster with your fingers, to eliminate air bubbles on the surface of the model. As the plaster slowly gets firmer, you can add handfuls of plaster to the pattern. Be patient with the plaster, working it on a time frame dictated by the plaster. Don't attempt to work too fast, or you will have liquid plaster all over your table.

Continue slowly adding plaster till the pattern is covered to a thickness of ½ to ¾ inch. Smooth the surface of the casting with a wide-blade knife. Make a smooth, flat, level surface on the top of the plaster. When the plaster is inverted for use as a negative mold, this flattened face makes a bed, keeping the mold level and steady.

Let the casting lie undisturbed till it becomes firm. Touch the casting occasionally as it cures to monitor its heat. It will probably take about 45 minutes for the casting to show signs of getting warm. As the heat reaches its peak, oil-based modeling clay softens. Separate the casting from the sculpture when the casting has started to cool. Separating plaster castings while the modeling clay is soft is especially important if there is even a hint of an undercut in the pattern.

Preparing the Mold

Prepare the plaster casting for use as a mold by cleaning stray slivers of modeling clay from it. The mold works best if you can let it set a few days in a warm place to dry. When excess water stored in the crystals of the plaster evaporates, the mold's absorption qualities are improved.

Safety Considerations

Neoprene casting rubber is not a dangerous product to use if you operate with some simple precautions.

The odors produced by neoprene are not harsh or offensive but beware of overexposure. The manufacturer indicates that vapors from neoprene should not be breathed. *Work outdoors or in a space where ventilation is provided to carry all vapors away.*

The manufacturer cautions that long term

skin contact can cause burns, and that eye damage is possible if the liquid is splashed into the eyes. *Wear latex gloves to protect your hands, and goggles to protect your eyes.* Skin contact should be followed by washing, and clothing contaminated with the liquid must be removed and laundered.

Pouring the Neoprene Casting

Pour the neoprene into the newly made negative plaster mold, filling it to within ½ inch of the brim. Neoprene is a very thin and weak looking liquid. It may surprise you to see what a tough, durable casting it becomes when it cures.

Give the plaster plenty of time to work the solvent out of the neoprene solution. The product we use takes about 2 hours to form a ³/₁₆ inch wall. Less time makes a thinner wall, more time will make a thicker, tougher wall. Don't let the thin wall fool you, however; cured neoprene is a very tough, durable material. It is not likely you would want a mask with a wall thicker than ³/₁₆ inch.

After the recommended two hours, pour the unabsorbed neoprene solution back into its jar to be used another time. If a thin skin forms as a result of air drying it can contaminate the batch. Remove the skin by absorbing it in a paper towel and discarding it. Turn the casting upside down for a while and allow it to drain; otherwise the liquid neoprene is likely to puddle in the nose, lips, and eyebrows, making them excessively thick.

Almost all of the neoprene solution you poured into the mold is recoverable. You encounter your biggest loss as you attempt to pour the surplus neoprene back into the jug. The stuff is so thin! The plaster mold is so unwieldy! No matter how you hold it, the liquid *just will* pour all over the table. A funnel helps—maybe a large funnel.

It is essential to store liquid neoprene in an airtight receptacle containing a minimum of air. A small air leak (or a small quantity of neoprene in a large container) allows the rubber to gel to a useless blob.

Opening the Mold

Wait another period of 6 to 10 hours (overnight is best) and the mask is ready to pull from the mold. In fact, it will already be shrinking slightly and pulling from the plaster sides.

Trimming the Mask
Trim the mask with a pair of scissors. Cut the eyes and nostrils with a mat knife or a chisel.

The casting still contains a good deal of solvent at this stage and it is very flexible. There is also a noticeable odor, which will take its leave in another day or so when the casting is fully cured.

Attaching a Head Strap
The attachment point for a head strap is usually right at the temples of the mask. Some formulas of hot glue bond tightly to neoprene and can connect a head strap made of elastic or cloth tape to the mask. We use formula 1942 made by Hysol. If you use glue, use plenty. A large glob carries heat to the joint, making it a more secure attachment.

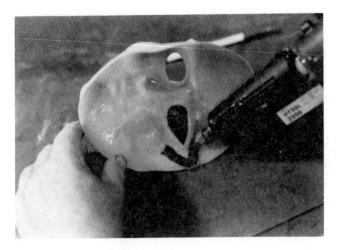

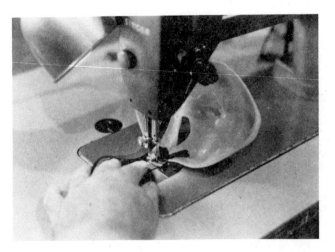

An alternative method of attachment consists of a metal loop and a short cloth strap. The strap doubles the area of contact for the glue to grip. Thread the strap through the metal loop and fasten both ends to the temple of the mask. Make

a similar attachment to the other temple.

The actual head strap is a length of ⅝ inch elastic band. Thread it through the same metal loops, fold it back onto itself, and sew it securely.

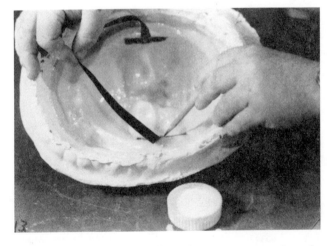

Embedding the cloth into the freshly poured neoprene casting is another excellent way to attach a strap to a neoprene mask. You must be prepared, however, to do the attachment as part of the casting procedure.

Cut the strap to the correct length and sew short tabs to each of the ends. This increases the

area of attachment and makes a stronger bond. Saturate the end of the cloth tape in liquid neoprene and attach the strap as soon as you pour the surplus neoprene from your mold. Press the wetted strap and its tabs into the soft, uncured neoprene casting. As the casting cures it unites with the strap.

Polishing the Surface of the Mask

You can smooth the surface of a neoprene mask by buffing it with a rag dipped in acetone. Small blemishes can even be removed when they are polished this way.

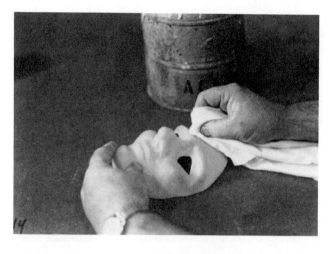

Painting the Mask

All kinds of paints adhere well to neoprene—lacquer, enamel, and acrylic. We used an airbrush to decorate these masks, applying the colors in a realistic way, almost as if it were a makeup job.

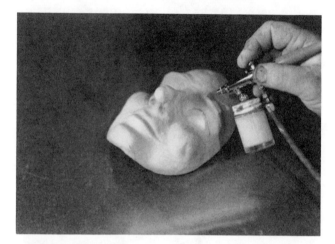

These masks appeared in the final scene of the 1988 UCLA production of *Much Ado About Nothing*. At dress rehearsal we realized the actresses had to be able to remove the masks without removing their veils. We replaced the head straps with sticks and the business was easily accomplished.

Kate Douvan designed this set of masks for *Takara No Tsuruhashi,* a play for children, set in Korea. We needed sixteen masks, all constructed on the same mold, but decorated differently. We chose to do them in neoprene, knowing that once our molds were made, the labor of producing the castings was minimal. We produced two molds to make the work go faster.

This photo shows the work in four different stages of progress.

1) A fresh pouring of neoprene in the plaster mold, during the 2-hour period when the mold leaches solvent from the liquid, making the walls of the casting.

2) A casting air drying so it can be removed from the plaster mold.

3) Four castings in need of trimming.

4) Three masks completely decorated.

This is a production photo of one of the gods—"Grandmother Water."

Thermoplastics

All thermoplastics have certain common characteristics — they soften when exposed to heat, they can be formed while they are soft, and they hold the new shape when they cool. Mask makers have used at least three different thermoplastic materials — Hexcelite, Friendly Plastic, and styrene in sheet form. These plastics all work on the thermoplastic principle, but they do not have much else in common. Friendly Plastic comes in bead form, works like a putty, and should be cast in a negative mold. Hexcelite is a plastic netting with 3/8 inch hexagonal holes. The mesh pattern gives this product a distinctive appearance. It forms equally well over a negative or positive mold. Styrene (and a few other plastics) come in large sheets, form best over a positive mold, and require the use of a vacuum-forming machine. These last two thermoplastics will be demonstrated in the next section on positive molds (page 79).

Friendly Plastic

Friendly Plastic is a trade name for one formulation of polyolefin. As its trade name implies, Friendly Plastic is fast and easy to use once you are familiar with a few simple techniques. Friendly Plastic is the hardest, least flexible mask-making material illustrated in this book. This thermoplastic softens at about 200°F., spreads like a putty in a negative mold, and solidifies at normal room temperatures. A mask made of this product can easily be made too thick and, if it becomes heavy, is inclined to shift with the performer's head movement. It is a hard, unyielding plastic and must, therefore, be fitted with some care to conform to face size.

The manufacturer suggests you use glass cookware, and that you shape the soft plastic to a workable size sheet with a rolling pin. The heated plastic looks and works a lot like taffy.

Heating the Plastic
Pour about a cupful of the Friendly Plastic beads into water you have placed on a heat source. If you have scraps of Friendly Plastic left over from another job, you can reheat them instead of using your supply of new material. One of the good features of a thermoplastic is that it is reusable.

Before the water reaches its boiling point the plastic will begin to melt. The beads (or chunks) become translucent as they soften and join together, forming a blob.

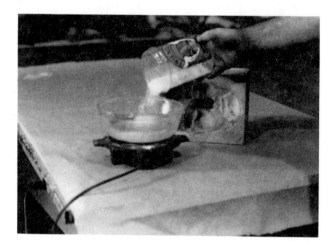

If you have ever attended a taffy pull, you will have a little advance understanding of the working characteristics of this plastic. The softened plastic has the consistency of salt water taffy.

Mold Releasing Agents

Water is a good release agent when you work with polyolefin. Soaking your plaster mold in water for a few minutes helps to keep the plastic casting from sticking to the plaster mold. Water would be enough if you could just keep the mold and your hands sloppy wet enough. Soon, however, a finger or two gets dry enough for the plastic to stick to you, and as with pulling taffy, things become quite unmanageable. Keep your hands clean and grease up your fingers and the mold just as you would at a taffy pull, but don't use butter.

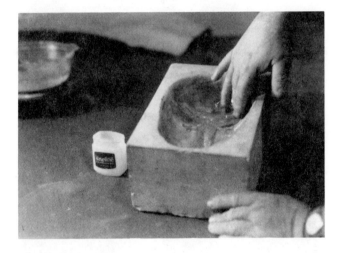

Coat the mold, your hands, your tools, and any part of your work space that may touch the hot plastic with some baby oil, vegetable oil, or petroleum jelly. Don't use much — a little oil goes a long way with this material.

While the plastic is heating, preheat your mold with a heat gun. A heated mold allows the casting to cool more slowly, and helps eliminate objectionable freeze lines where the applications of plastic overlap.

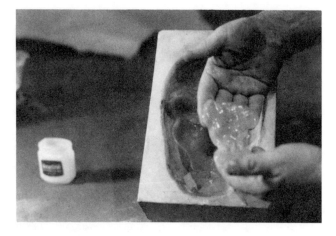

At first, the softened glob is too hot to handle. Allow it to cool in the air for a few minutes and you will to be able to stand the heat and work it in your hands. Make a plastic pancake.

Filling the Mold

Make a patty of plastic about ¼ inch thick and four or five inches in diameter. Lay this pancake into the heated mold and press it into all of the depressions. Spread it to cover a larger area by carefully forcing the plastic to a uniform thickness of ⅛ to ³/₁₆ inches. Work as quickly and efficiently as you can, but as slowly as you must, finishing the casting as you go. Conform to all the features of the mold and try hard to maintain a uniform thickness.

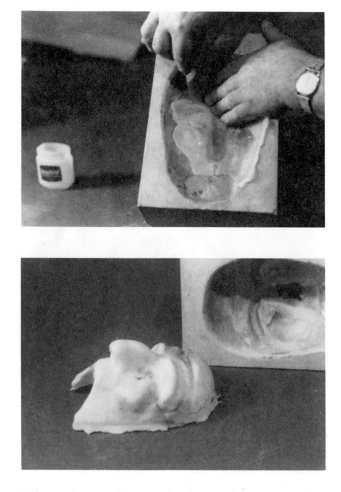

Get another wad of the plastic, and let it air cool till you can handle it. Make a pancake, and apply it to the mold, slightly overlapping it into the previous coating. Ideally, the first application will still be warm and soft, so a good bond can be formed. Five or six applications should fill a normal sized mask mold.

When the casting cools, becoming an opaque white, you can lift it from the mold. The separation should be effortless if there are no undercuts.

Examine the casting for freeze lines — places that have not joined smoothly because of too rapid cooling. This casting has several, but they refused to disclose themselves in the photograph. We therefore doctored the mask with stain to make the flaws more obvious in the photo.

Correcting Freeze Lines

Correct freeze lines by heating the surface of the plastic with a heat gun to its softening point. This point can be reached very quickly if you hold the gun close to the surface. Wet a finger with water and test the temperature of the plastic. When it is cool enough to touch, polish the freeze lines away with your finger.

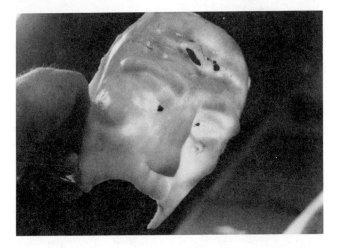

Thin spots in the casting can be detected by holding the mask in front of a strong light. Holes become grossly apparent, and thin spots show as transparent areas.

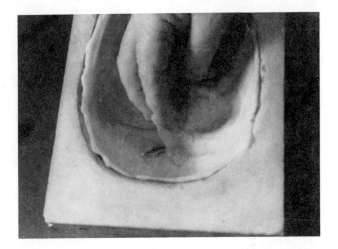

Repair the holes and thin spots by replacing the mask form in the mold and filling it with silver dollar-sized pancakes of freshly heated plastic. The patch melts into the casting, but freeze lines remain and must be dealt with.

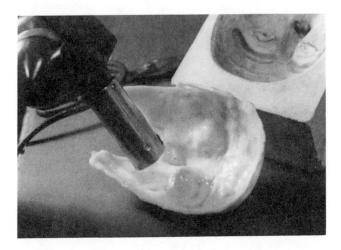

Make the bond complete and eliminate freeze lines as you did before by carefully heating the

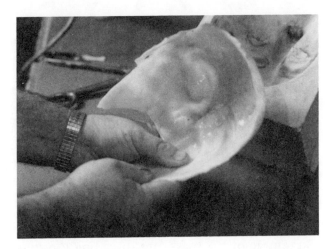

surface and polishing the joint with a wetted thumb or finger.

Trimming the Mask

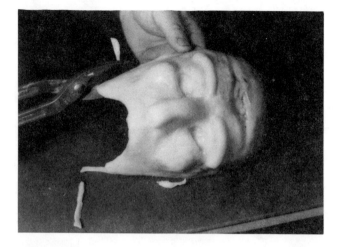 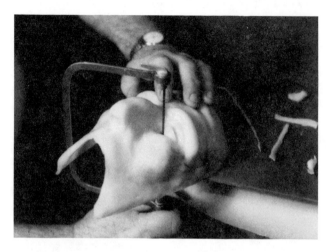

Trim the perimeter of the mask with tin snips. Friendly Plastic in thicknesses greater than ⅛ inch is very tough and may not even respond to your efforts with metal shears—you may have to use a wood saw. A coping saw easily opens the eyes of the mask. Rough edges left from any of these cuts can be effectively removed by polishing them with a heat gun and a wetted finger. Save the scraps. They can be reheated and used on your next casting.

Attaching a Headband

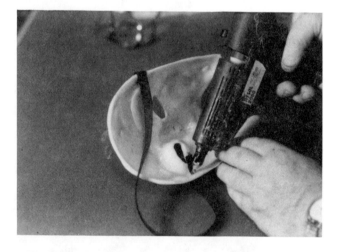 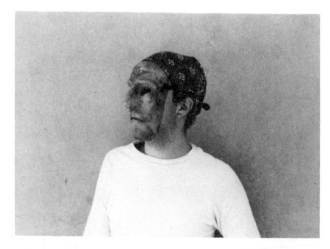

Attach an elastic head strap by drilling a hole near the temple of the mask and threading the strap through it. Use hot glue to bond the strap to the plastic mask. Hot glue, also a formulation of polyolefin, is an especially good bonding agent to use with this product.

This mask was built as one of a series of character masks for acting class exercises.

MAKING A POSITIVE GYPSUM CEMENT MOLD

Vacuum-formed styrene, Celastic, orthopaedic casting tape, and leather are all mask-making materials that work best over a positive form.

Fortunately, there is a way to make a hard positive mold directly from a negative plaster mold.

Waste Mold

As a matter of practice, mold makers try to construct flexible castings from a rigid mold, such as plaster. We have just demonstrated how to cast neoprene and latex in a plaster mold. The plan of casting with these flexible materials is perfectly consistent with this practice. The pliant casting can pull away from the hard mold, even where there are slight undercuts, something a rigid cast-ing would be unable to do. On the next few pages we will demonstrate how to separate a posi-tive casting of gypsum cement by breaking away the rigid plaster negative mold with a hammer. The violent action is not the aftermath of mis-calculation; it is planned from the beginning, and as a result the mold is called a "waste mold."

Preparing the Mold
Fill imperfections in the negative form (air bub-bles, scars made by release agent, etc.) with a commercial spackling paste, a paste you make

from a small amount of fresh plaster, or you might even use clay.

Apply petroleum jelly or soap to the negative mold to act as a release agent.

Mixing and Using Gypsum Cement

Mix up a batch of Hydrocal. For a mold this size you need about a half gallon. Hydrocal is a trade name of the United States Gypsum Co., and is not a plaster product. It is a gypsum cement, setting up harder and much more permanently than plaster.

Mix the Hydrocal in almost the same way you would mix a batch of plaster. (See Mixing and Using Plaster on page 57.) There is one major

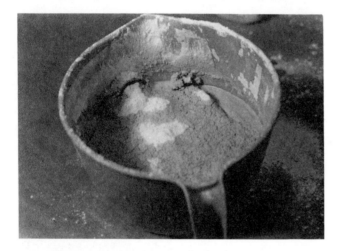

Pouring the Casting

Invert your mold, securing it solidly to the work table. Put a firm base of modeling clay under the mold if it seems to be at all unsteady.

Set the mold aside for an overnight curing period.

difference, however; gypsum cements require less water than plaster. The manufacturer recommends a mixing ration of 5 parts water to 10 parts powder (by weight). Therefore, you must put about ⅓ less water into your mixing pan before adding the powder. If you begin with the same amount of water as you did in mixing the plaster, you would certainly have more cement than you intended.

Sift the Hydrocal powder into the water till no more is accepted. Let the mixture sit without stirring for five minutes or so as to soak into the powder, till it is moistened completely. The mix should look like it does in the photo: the surface should be mostly covered with damp powder. There can be a few pools of liquid around the edges of the mixing pan.

Stir the mixture of Hydrocal thoroughly. A small batch can be mixed with your hands, but best results (harder, more durable molds) are obtained when you mix with an electrically driven mixer. The mixing method suggested here yields a blend that can be poured easily. Pour the mix into the mold, filling it to the brim. Tap the mold repeatedly. Vibrating the mold shakes air bubbles from the face of the mold, and encourages them to rise to the surface of the liquid.

Opening the Mold

Take a hammer and break away the plaster mold. Direct the blows to the edges of the inverted plaster mold, *knocking them away from the Hydrocal*

Vigorous pounding on a negative mold with *deep* undercuts, however, could break the positive casting. The nostrils on this large nose have excessive undercuts. When you know this in advance you can be prepared to deal with the problem.

Do not start at the outside and chip away at the edges. This is a very messy technique as the small plaster pieces splatter all over your shop. Rather, direct the blows of the chisel to the center of the underlying casting. Run a series of small cuts in a line, always holding the chisel perpendicular to the center of the mass of the casting.

casting. If there are no deep undercuts, this technique is straightforward and recommended.

A soft plaster mold made with thin walls breaks much more easily than a hard, thick, solid gypsum cement casting.

In these instances, a cold chisel can be very helpful. After you knock away the easy outside edges by hitting them with a hammer, you can finish the job with a cold chisel, but be careful to use it in the right way.

The mold breaks cleanly down the center and falls apart freely on both sides of the undercut.

Finishing the Positive Mold

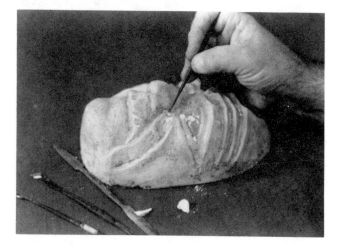 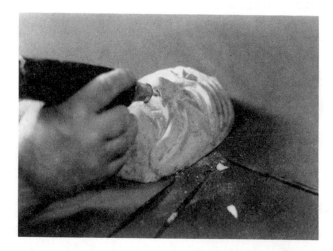

The Hydrocal casting should be perfect and ready for use as a positive mask-making mold. Or it can be worked, smoothed, and refined with files, dental tools, and sandpaper. Or, if you feel there is a need, the features could be greatly modified with an electric grinding tool such as a Dremel.

CASTING A MASK OVER A POSITIVE MOLD

The remainder of this book will deal with techniques of working mask-making materials over a positive mold. Styrene, Celastic, glue cloth, and leather are thin bodied and flexible, so they can be shaped very well on a positive form. It is true that you may lose some of the very finest details that can be designed into the mold. Wrinkles and ridges smaller than 3/16 inch will probably not reproduce in the finished mask (because of the thickness of the casting material), but this is simply a limitation of the medium you are working with. You are well advised to eliminate details this small from your mask design, or if you feel they are absolutely necessary, add them with paint.

Vacuum-formed Styrene

If speed is your greatest concern, use a vacuum-forming machine to reproduce complete sets of masks all at one time. Of course, in order for this process to have any validity for you, you must have such a machine at your disposal. But if you do, it's fast.

The Vacuum-forming Operation

There are two major parts to the machine—an oven and a forming table. Prepare the forming table by placing the positive plaster mask pattern on its surface. Clamp a sheet of 40 mil white high impact styrene into a frame and lay it onto the oven to soften it.

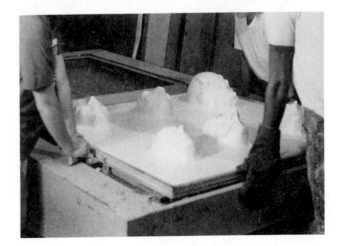

Within a few minutes, the plastic sheet will become soft and rubbery. The operators flip the frame and the plastic it holds, transferring it to the forming table and its patterns. They immediately apply the vacuum, which presses the plastic tightly to the pattern. The resulting thin plastic shells are very near replicas of the original mold.

The machine in these photos will mass produce, forming the masks at the rate of six at one time.

Trimming the Plastic Castings

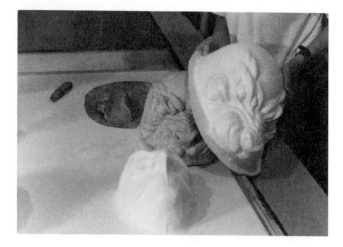

Cut the thin plastic shell from the table with a mat knife. The mask can then be trimmed with either the knife or a pair of scissors.

Attaching Head Straps
At this stage the mask has much of the quality one finds in a dime store Halloween mask. It has a thicker body, to be sure, but is reminiscent nonetheless. An elastic headband could be stapled in place (in keeping with the dime store model) or you might make it more secure by hot gluing the strap in position.

Acrylic paints or any number of different trimmings can be applied to the styrene for decoration. You will find some specific ideas for decorating these masks in the section on Decorating Techniques (page 95).

Half Masks of Vacuum-formed Styrene

Five of the court ladies carried vizards (a half mask on a stick) in our 1989 production of *The Changeling*.

We already had a positive form that had been taken from a life mask in stock. It was decided, under the circumstances, that the efficient way to produce five reproductions of the same mask design was to use the vacuum-forming process.

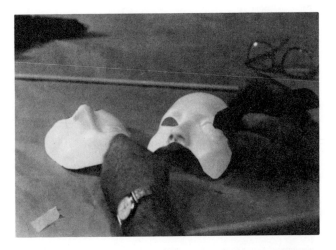

We made five copies of the mask in 40 mil styrene. Using a felt marker, we traced the perimeter of the border. Then we cut the outline with a mat knife.

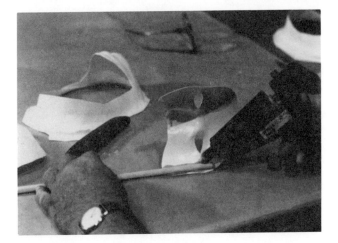

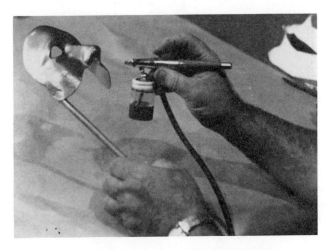

Hot glue was used to attach a 24-inch stick to the side of the styrene mask. Finally, the mask was sprayed with a high gloss enamel paint.

Pomp and convention were much more important than disguise as these half masks were in use.

Thermoplastic Orthopaedic Tape

Recently, a product has appeared on the market that was designed for the medical profession, but is finding wide use in the theater for construction of both costumes and properties. The product is too new to have picked up a good generic name, so it is usually known by one of its trade names, "Hexcelite." One of the more obvious theatrical uses has been the making of stylized masks.

Hexcelite can be purchased in large sheets from the manufacturer, but it is more easily obtained in small quantities in the form of rolls, packaged as orthopaedic tape. Although this tape is packaged for doctors to set broken bones, it is a plastic material, and has nothing to do with plaster.

Heating the Tape

The mesh of the Hexcelite is filled with a thermoplastic resin. This plastic becomes soft when it is exposed to heat (about 150°F.) and hardens when it is cooled to room temperature.

The strips can be softened with either dry or wet heat. One convenient way to heat the material is to drop it in water which is just below the boiling point, for 3 to 4 minutes.

Shaping the Tape

When the open weave fabric is removed from the water it readily loses its heat, soon becoming comfortable to the touch and still remaining quite soft and workable. The fabric can be stretched and molded to conform to the shape of any ready-made form or pattern.

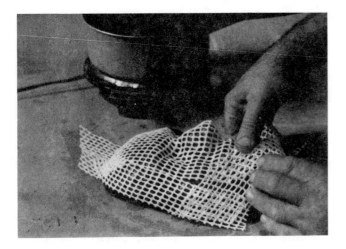

The strips can be crisscrossed and built up in layers to completely cover the surface of your pattern. The softened plastic will adhere to itself as the layers are placed one on top of another.

Spot Treating and Splicing the Tape
Dry heat from a hair dryer or a heat gun can also be used to "spot weld" any point that might need it. Spot heating the plastic mesh will tend to melt it into the surface of your pattern, so a mold release of Teflon spray, silicone spray, or aluminum foil should be used between these surfaces.

It takes less than 10 minutes to make a Hexcelite copy of a form as small as a mask. Since this operation is so very fast, it is possible to produce this style of mask in quantity.

This half mask was made from a single piece of mesh. Metallic ribbons were woven through the loose weave of the plastic fabric.

Celastic

After World War II, a young plastics industry gave the theater an easy to work casting material with the trade name "Celastic." The techniques of handling Celastic for mask making are very much like those used in working with papier-mâché, and the finished masks have a very similar appearance. These materials are, however, worlds apart chemically, Celastic being stronger and thus, more durable. The person already familiar with papier-mâché can be immediately successful with this product.

Celastic is made of a cloth fabric which has been entirely filled with cellulose nitrate. Medium weight Celastic has the consistency of thin cardboard and can be torn into strips before it is treated with the solvent. When it is soaked in the proper solvent, the cellulose nitrate dissolves and becomes very soft and workable. As the solvent evaporates, the cloth becomes rigidly stiff, retains its shape, and is no longer affected by the actions of a solvent.

The qualities of Celastic that make it a good mask-making material are these: it is lightweight and the strength-to-weight ratio is high. A mask made of medium grade Celastic, two or three layers thick, is very durable. Such a mask becomes stiff and abrasive, however, and must be lined with felt or cushioned with foam rubber in order to be comfortable on the performer's face.

Safety Considerations

Acetone is a widely used solvent for Celastic. It is flammable and dangerous in the presence of sparks or flames. Acetone fumes are harmful to lung tissue and can produce dizziness and headache. It should not be used without adequate ventilation. Methyl-ethyl-ketone (MEK) was once the recommended solvent to use with Celastic, but it is much more toxic, and has been linked to permanent neurological damage. Do not use MEK. Acetone is a skin irritant and should not be used without protecting your hands with barrier lotion or rubber gloves.

Making a Celastic Casting

Petroleum jelly works pretty well as a release agent between Celastic and plaster. However, if you are not careful, the solvent in Celastic (acetone) may reduce the effectiveness of the mold release. The first coating of Celastic should not be excessively wet as it is applied. Put it on rather dry, and do not rub the first coat, or the acetone will dilute the petroleum jelly.

Find a well ventilated work space and pour out a shallow pan of acetone. Tear up a supply of Celastic strips. The strips should average about 1″ × 2″ in order to pick up details normally found in mask making. The strips should be torn and not snipped with a pair of scissors. A torn edge will make a smoother "feather-edged" blend into its neighbor than would be possible with the hard-cut edge made by a pair of scissors.

Dip a few strips of Celastic in the solvent and let them soak. Soaking loosens the plastic filler in the fabric and makes it more workable, allowing for a smoother blend where the strips overlap. A word of caution, however: if you leave the strip in the solvent too long, all of the plastic will float out of the fabric.

Lay the first strip into the mask form and rub it with your fingers, making it conform to the contours of the mold. Get another wetted strip, run it between your crossed fingers to wring out the extra solvent, and crisscross it into the previous one.

Generously overlap the strips, massaging the softened plastic filler into the adjoining fabric with your finger, forcing the strips to blend together. Continue in this way until the mold is completely coated with crisscrossing layers of softened plastic strips. You will need to prepare smaller strips of Celastic to capture the more intricate details of the mask. Broad, flat areas (foreheads, cheeks, etc.) can be covered with larger pieces, but don't allow a large strip to produce an objectionable fold. A mask constructed of one single coating of crisscrossed Celastic strips will be at least two layers thick in most places and very strong.

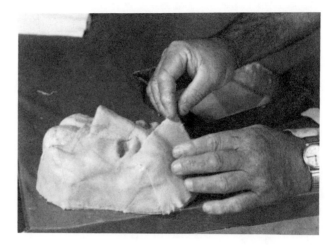

If you apply another coating of Celastic to the mold, you would certainly make the mask more durable. Indeed, you may want to add another coating of strips around the perimeter of the mask to strengthen it there. But there is reason for concern if you make the entire mask too thick.

The build-up of the fabric may bridge over some of the finer details that you sculpted into the positive original.

The thickness of the Celastic fabric produces a certain roughness on the surface where the pieces overlap.

One technique of reducing this unevenness has already been mentioned—that of polishing the edges with a finger wetted in acetone. Another highly effective method of blending these overlaps is to use a wad of Celastic that has been thoroughly saturated in acetone. The plastic transfers from the polishing wad to the seam, bridging across the layers and filling up most of the unevenness.

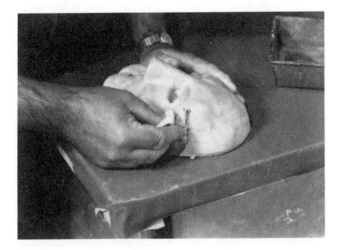

Be patient with this process, wetting with acetone as necessary, polishing the edges, until finally you have nothing left in your fingers to polish with but a limp rag. Continue the process till the entire surface of the mask is as smooth as you can get it.

Let the mold rest overnight. The solvent will evaporate, and you will be left with a hard-shelled mask.

The next day, pull the Celastic casting from its mold. It should be hard and dry. If it is dry, or almost dry, you can begin to finish it and trim the edges. If, on the other hand, the casting is still damp and at all flimsy, put it back into the mold and give it some more time. Be patient.

Trim the outline of the mask with a mat knife or a pair of tin snips. Carefully design the eye shape and the nostrils, sketching the outlines with a pencil. Cut these open with a sharp mat knife also.

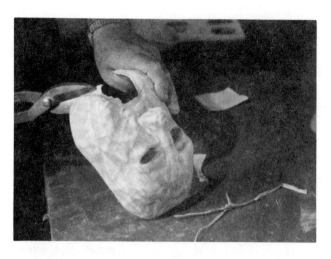

When the mask is dry, the surface can be treated in a final attempt at removing surface unevenness. The degree of finishing of the rough surface will depend on how you choose to decorate the finished mask. If you plan to use paint, sand the hard Celastic with a fine grade sandpaper, feathering the edges of any strip that might still be showing its individuality. If you decide to decorate with a cloth or fur covering (see the Decorating Techniques on page 95), the surface can be used rough, just as it comes from the mold.

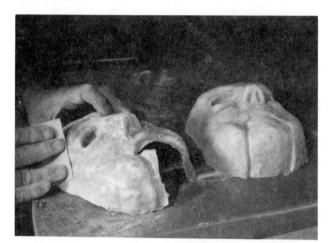

A strap outfitted with Velcro fasteners can be secured to the mask by embedding the strap in fresh coatings of Celastic. Apply newly wetted strips of the plastic to both sides of the straps, then press them in place just above the temple on both sides of the mask.

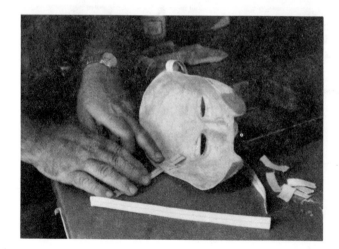

Glue Cloth

This process is a not too distant cousin to papier-mâché. You work over a positive mask mold rather than a negative one, substitute a light-bodied stretchable fabric (jersey or spandex) for the paper, and use a flexible bookbinder's glue instead of the hard PVA white glue. The result is that the mask will be flexible (in thin coats it can be even more flexible than latex rubber). An unsupported mask may sag and lose its features till it is again backed with a suitable foundation — the performer's face will do nicely.

If you use a natural colored stretch facric, the unpainted mask has some of the quality of muslin, and works in an interesting way with a loose pajama-like costume. There is a smooth, unobtrusive transition between the costume and the performer's face.

We have selected an animal face for the mask form on this project. The positive form was made of Hydrocal, but plaster or any firm material would work for the mold.

Mold Release
Flex glue clings tenaciously to most materials, but is naturally releasing from several others. Crêpe backed, Scotch brand masking tape is one of these. Apply an even coating of masking tape to the entire surface of the mold. Use small pieces of tape, crossing and overlapping them as they are applied. Rub the edges of the tape with your finger to make them lie smoothly on the mold's surface.

Applying the First Coat
Lay the fabric on the mold and begin to paint the surface with a coating of flex glue. Leave lots of fullness in the fabric as it is applied.

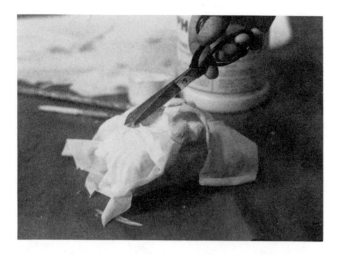

Try to cover the mask form with one uncut sheet of fabric, even though it is unlikely that you will be successful. Folds will form in some places and air gaps will form in others. These flaws can be eliminated if you cut the fabric. The overlaps will not show in the final product. Cut the cloth and overlap the edges where it is necessary. Glue down the loose edges.

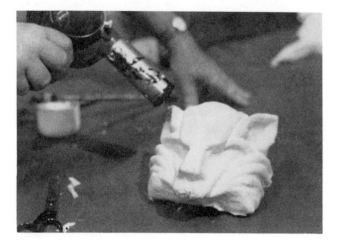

Force dry the first layer with gentle heat from a hot air gun or a hair dryer. The hot air forms a skin over the outer face of the glue-coated fabric. You will be able to work on the surface of this skin, and not get your fingers stuck in the un-cured glue below.

Run your fingers over the freshly skinned surface. Look for air gaps and thick layers that may have formed in the cloth. Press on these places to force the fabric even closer to the mask form.

Applying the Second Coat

When the material is as nearly like the mold as possible, begin the process again to make a second coat. Lay on another piece of fabric, paint it with glue, and allow lots of fullness to fall into the contours. Cut and overlap sections where folds exist, put small pieces where voids may have formed, force dry a surface skin, and work the skin with your fingers until it is smooth and form fitting.

Let the mask set overnight so it can dry completely.

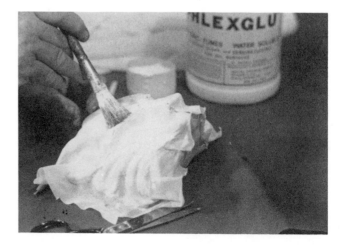

Trimming the Mask

As you trim the perimeter of the form, leave a little surplus around the rim of the mask. Your cut should be about ½ inch larger than the planned edge of the mask. This ½ inch edging will be folded back and glued in place to add strength to the border of the mask.

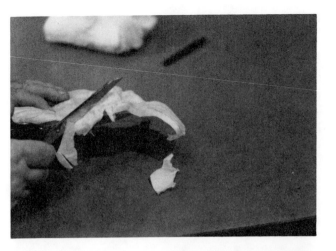

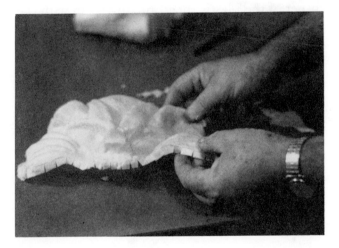

Cut slits in the border to relieve stress and allow the edging to fold flat. Use flex glue to hold the hem in place.

It may be necessary to return the mask to the positive form till the glue from this operation has dried.

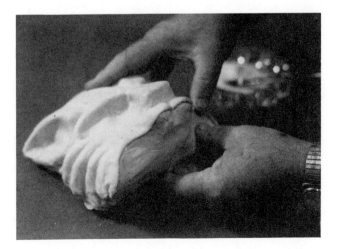

Painting the Mask

The completed mask can be painted or treated with a variety of finishes. We have chosen to use a brown dye mixed with the same flex glue to act as a binder. The glue-dye mixture can be brushed smoothly onto the surface, or it could be daubed on as we did.

We are using a sheet of plastic as a drop cloth, because flex glue peels away cleanly from most plastic materials. You can make a palette for the dyes (in this case a brown and a blue) on one corner of the plastic sheet, mixing them with the flex glue. When the glue dries, this dye puddle can be peeled away and discarded.

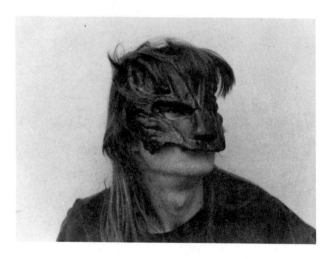

DECORATING TECHNIQUES

The mask-making materials we have met on the preceding pages can be ornamented with a great variety of materials. Paints, dyes, sequins, feathers, fabrics, foils, ribbons, jewels, bells, furs, hair, wigs, etc. all have their place in decorating a specific mask. But the down side of this is that a mask's material loses the positive effect of its unique surface texture as soon as you start hanging decorations on it. In fact, it is unlikely that you could identify the material that a completely decorated mask was crafted from without turning it over and looking at the reverse. If the interior of the mask has been covered with flannel or felt (as it sometimes is, to improve comfort), you are really at a loss.

You should be successful in finishing a mask made from Friendly Plastic, Celastic, papier-mâché, neoprene, or vacuum-formed styrene using any of the following techniques of decoration.

Covering a Mask with Fabric

Covering a mask with shiny fabric is one very effective method of decoration. These masks were made of vacuum-formed styrene, but you will have similar results working over any hard, smooth, unbending surface. Choose a cloth that is capable of stretching, such as spandex or jersey. Using a stretch fabric allows you to cover the mask in one seamless piece.

Applying the Cloth

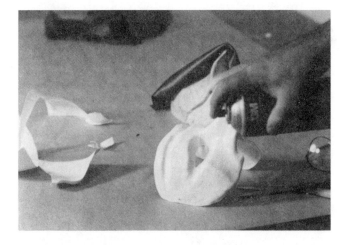

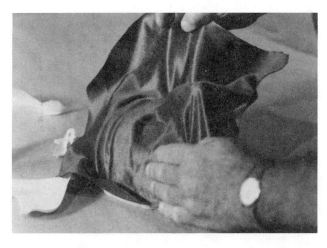

Spray the entire surface of the mask with a heavy coating of spray adhesive.

Let the mask air dry till there are no moist spots remaining. The entire surface must be tacky. If the cement is liquid when the cloth makes contact, it spots the fabric, and adhesion will not readily occur.

Lay the stretchy fabric into the bed of tacky adhesive. Force an ample amount of fullness to fall into the lowest of the depressions. Providing fullness in all the low spots is more important than may at first be obvious.

Do not rely on the stretchable character of the fabric as your only means of making the cloth conform to the features of the mask — you simply will not be successful. Tension on the fabric becomes greater than the adhesive power of the cement. The fabric slowly pulls away, forming air pockets between the cloth and the styrene.

Still, wrinkles may form in the extreme contours of the mask despite your most careful attention. You may have to split the fabric and allow it to overlap. Make the incision as short as possible — near a perimeter or eye hole.

Trimming and Finishing Edges

Trim the cloth with a pair of scissors, leaving a border of surplus material about ½ inch from the outer edge of the mask.

Cut slits in the surplus cloth to make gluing tabs. You will need more of these slits at the corners and on curves than on the sides where the line is straight.

Spray a heavy coating of adhesive on the tabs and the edges of the mask where the tabs will fall. Let the glue air dry till it is tacky.

Press the tabs down, making the perimeter of the mask smooth and neat.

These masks have been covered with spandex, decorated with raised ribbons from a hot glue gun, painted in places with acrylic paints, and trimmed with rhinestones. They were prepared for the ballroom scene in our 1988 production of *Romeo and Juliet*.

Covering a Mask with Animal Fur

You can build a durable animal mask by gluing fur over a positive form. The procedure is demonstrated on vacuum-formed styrene, but any mask form that is rigid enough to supply the required support will work fine. The process is almost (but not quite) a duplicate of the technique just demonstrated. The mask produced is wondrously different.

Preparing the Skin

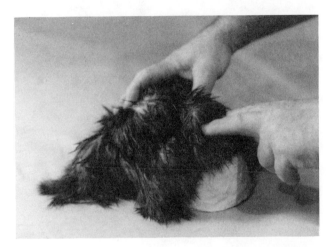

Saturate the fur in warm water. Wring out all the surplus water and lay the fur on your positive mask mold. We have chosen a pattern that contains animal features for our mold.

Spend some time and effort pushing on the flexible skin, making it conform to the shape of the underlying plaster mold. When the form dries, the skin holds a very limp memory of this shape. It will need to be reinforced, and that is what we are about to do in this project.

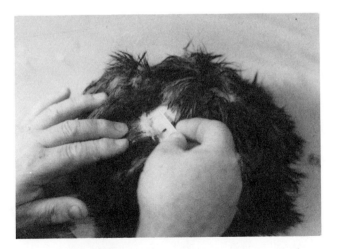

Locate the eye placement and, while the skin is still water soaked, shave a small spot over each eye, free from fur.

Give the fur a gentle grooming and let it lie alone all night to dry.

Supporting the Fur

Make a mask form from any of the harder rigid materials we have covered: neoprene, papiermâché, styrene, Friendly Plastic, or Celastic. The illustrations show vacuum-formed styrene being used.

Spray the styrene with rubber adhesive.

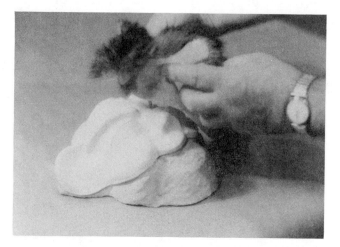

Lay the fur on the mask form while the adhesive is still wet. Waiting till the adhesive is dry and tacky makes it difficult to adjust the fur, if your first attempt at placement is slightly misaligned.

Trim the edges, open the eyes, and the rabbit fur has become a dog. Or is it a bear?

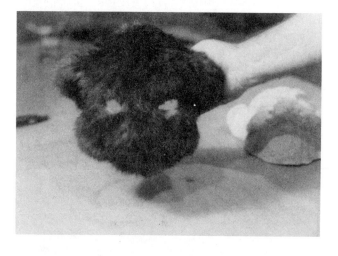

Simulating a Metal Finish

Gold Leaf

This mask was made of Friendly Plastic, but any hard surface can be covered with gold leaf. Give the mask a heavy coating of spray adhesive and let it dry.

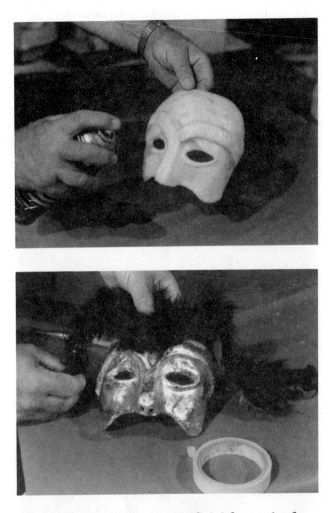

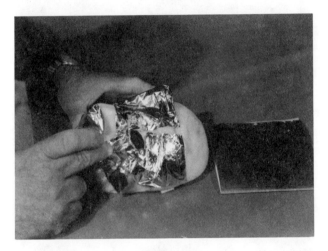

Lay the gold leaf into the tacky surface, and press the foil gently with your fingers. Come back with a second application of foil to cover the splits and voids. After the adhesive has had time to dry, brush away the excess pieces of foil.

We decided to glue some artificial fur to the forehead of this mask to act as stylized hair.

Metallic Tape

There are several metallic tapes on the market that have an adhesive backing. These stick with fervor to a smooth, hard surface such as that of the mask shown, which was cast in neoprene.

Random overlaps necessarily occur as you cover the surface with tape. But the tape is thin enough that the overlaps do not show objectionably unless your design requires a polished appearance.

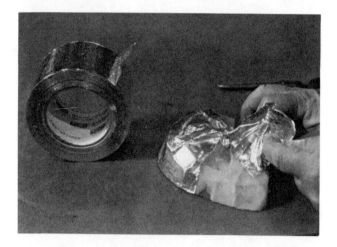

The slight fault at the overlap completely disappears if you texture the mask. Adding a patina to the metallic surface with dyes is one way of providing such a texture.

These masks have been treated to make them assume a metallic appearance. The one on the right has an application of gold foil, the left is covered with aluminum tape, and the one in the center was wrapped with gold tape.

LEATHER MASKS AND THE COMMEDIA DELL'ARTE

*Signor Universo, one of Sartori's leather working craftsmen,
spraying dye onto a mask of Arlecchino.*

Leather mask making is inextricably associated with the commedia dell'arte characters of 16th and 17th century Italy. We cannot assume that all of their masks were crafted from leather, but there is plenty of evidence that leather was the standard.

In the section that follows we offer an interpretation of the major characters of the commedia dell'arte. Then, the remainder of this book will be devoted to an explanation of how to construct this set of commedia masks from leather.

If you have no interest in the commedia, but want to get on with leather mask making, you may skip the next few pages and begin. Forgive us if the examples used to demonstrate these techniques are those of the commedia characters.

A JOURNEY TO THE BEGINNINGS OF COMMEDIA DELL'ARTE

Come on a journey nearly seven centuries into the past. The world is struggling to be reborn from the dark days of the Middle Ages. We look in on a province in central Italy to witness the beginnings of that which will grow up in another 150 years to be commedia dell'arte. It is market day.

There is a carnival atmosphere in this early morning marketplace. Street vendors hawk their wares from booths or open air displays. You can hear them bartering and haggling with their customers at high volumes. The women meet in the streets and gossip as they shop. Children jostle, shout, and get under foot. Old men congregate and discuss local news. The homeless are present in abundance; the most unfortunate of these working the only trade they know—begging. The sounds of animals—those caged in the vendor booths and the domestic animals running free in the town square—add to the clamor. Street performers, acrobats, jugglers, clowns, and magicians vie with each other for the attention and the meager living that might be gleaned from the market day crowd. It is in this hustle of activity that a new art form struggles to be born.

There are two classes of people in this time and place: the peasants (the very poor) and the aristocracy (the very rich). The marketplace is heavily populated with the poor, but at times the wealthy make their appearance.

In the midst of the crowd we see a solo street performer. Indeed we cannot miss him—he does everything within his power to attract attention. This clever actor's sole purpose is to entertain, to be funny. His livelihood depends on his ability

Note: The author borrowed this fanciful account, tracing the roots of the commedia dell'arte, from a lecture delivered at UCLA by Italy's foremost contemporary interpreter of Arlecchino, Ferruccio Soleri, when he visited the United States in 1987.

to attract, amuse, and hold the attention of his crowd. The bigger the crowd, the bigger his income when he walks through his audience, hat in hand. He lives by his wits and his audacity.

Our performer cannot afford to be subtle in this beehive arena. Every aspect of his performance is bigger than life. His gestures are broad—meant to attract attention. He uses both his arms and his legs to gesture and to convey his story. And the movement is almost constant. He dances his story as much as tells it, accenting his punch lines with acrobatics. The concept of a street clown is not unique to this time and place. Something, however, *is* special here: the viewing public extends an appreciation which allows this work to develop.

To emphasize his broad comic effect, and to differentiate this act from others on the street, our performer has made a mask to exaggerate some facial features. He has been careful to enlarge on the features that will heighten the comic effect.

An enlarged nose—now that's funny! A mole, a wart, some wrinkles, or a carbuncle—yes—and some well placed facial hair. (A deformed mouth or eye would not do. Such a deformity would be grotesque, receiving pity rather than laughs.) Ah, but a nose...He designs the nose of the mask to be the main feature. It begins at the cheekbones and tapers to a point about 9 to 10 inches in front of his face.

In Italy, in the 14th century, Giovanni was a very common name, just as John was common 650 years later in America. Everyone is "Giovanni," especially a clown. "Gionni" (Johnny) the audience calls him. Gionni soon slurs into "Zanni," and the comic character receives a name by public acclaim.

These comic skits became greatly popular. Our street clown could never become wealthy, but he could enjoy local fame and reputation.

With time, he refined the characterization he created. His repertoire of clever narratives expanded and, the greatest compliment of all, he was imitated. The audience looked forward with anticipation to Zanni's next performance. The ground was fertile and receptive to the art of this new strain of street performer. And the seed of commedia dell'arte took root.

The stories were portrayed in the form of pantomime and monologue. They dealt with subjects with which market day peasants could intimately relate. Three basic themes recurred:

1. Love and sex. The pretty girl and how one might attain her affections—honorably or otherwise.

2. Money. Or rather, the important thing that money could provide to the poor class—food. The empty stomach was a subject with which all street people could identify.

3. Relationships between the servant and the master.

The Costume

The costume of these earliest street comics consisted of pants and blouse. Economy dictated that the clothing be large—one size fits all. The fabric was white—the inexpensive color. Dyeing fabric into gay colors cost money. The zanni had a hat that came to a double pointed bill in front with plumes. Feathers were plentiful and common at this time. The peasants lived with several kinds of birds and animals, and could pick feathers from molting birds directly from the ground.

The Mask

Zanni created his first mask to produce a comic effect. He wore it as an attention getter more than anything else, but it quickly evolved into much more. The exaggerated features allowed an audience to recognize a popular character immediately. In fact, the mask (the new face the actor donned on beginning his performance) was very soon identified with the *masque* (the character being portrayed). The mask standardized Zanni's appearance and, with time, various performers began to portray the same popular comic personality.

Remarkably, the mask did not hinder the speech of these performers. The half mask with a large nasal cavity resounded as the actor spoke, amplifying his voice.

Soon, two zannis got together. They realized that, through cooperation, a short scene could be played, and an exchange of dialogue added to the interest of their story.

Both of these characters were of the servant class. One developed to be the cleverest and funniest. He got all the good lines and situations. The other was the second comic and set up the jokes. The character we now know as Brighella is a descendant of the first comic, the quick witted, astute, sly, and crafty one. Arlecchino has his roots in his slower, simple, straight man, getting his laughs by being naive and childlike.

The next character to develop (it was likely a simultaneous development) was that of "The Magnifico"—the master. This character is old, wealthy, and miserly. His treatment of his servants is outrageous, but in these scenarios, invented as they are by the poor class, the master is served with a liberal dose of disrespect and deception. The master–servant scenario again provides the two performers the benefits of working together.

Several of the commedia dell'arte characters trace their ancestry back to 200 B.C. to the Roman comedy dramatists Plautus and Terence. The Magnifico is one of these. He and his descendant, "Pantalone," find many of their mannerisms in the character of Euclio from Plautus' *Aulularia*.

Pantalone has an eye for women. Fantasizing that they have an interest in him, he willingly allows the young girls to make a fool of him. Their only interest is the gold in his purse.

So it is that women were included in the scenarios, but not allowed to participate in the earliest performances. Young girls were played by men, masked to portray exaggerated beauty.

In this world of two widely separated classes (wealthy and poor), there were pretenders. A poor man could become a soldier for a wealthy lord and pretend to have climbed above his station. A mercenary had all the signs of wealth. He had food, beautiful clothes, a sword, and with a swagger and the inflated ego these bring, he could pretend to be wealthy. This character was a natural for exaggeration and on stage he began in Plautus' *Braggart Warrior.* This character became the model for "Il Capitano."

Another pretender is the professor or the doctor. Although he is truly a member of the aristocracy, he wants more. "Il Dottore" pretends to be better than his fellows because of his learning.

So, without anybody actually planning it, a company of four to six male actors was assembled. They played in their hometown for a time and then, as circumstances demanded it, they moved to a neighboring town in search of a new audience. Wandering from town to town became a way of life, and a troupe of traveling players was born.

A band of touring performers would undoubtedly have women in their party. Wives and girlfriends could not be left at home. It is not difficult to imagine how these women became a part of the performance. This short scenario was probably acted out many times backstage.

GIRLFRIEND: Why couldn't I play the part of the woman?

ZANNI: What do you know about the theater?

GIRLFRIEND: What do you know about being a woman?

Once the logic of this argument sank in, the first woman entered the commedia scene.

The performances were not scripted, but were based on the narratives and dialogues (*lazzi*) which had been learned and practiced when the actors were working solo or in groups of two. The subject matter of all these sketches was similar, so it was no trick for the manager of the company to weave a scenario or several scenarios from the specialty pieces that each performer brought with him.

The commedia dell'arte grew slowly from its rudimentary beginnings, took a recognizable form in 1550, and flourished in Italy for the next 200 years. Some other important characters were created: Pedrolino, Pulcinella, and Tartaglia to name a few. Other characters evolved by splintering off those that were successful. Pedrolino (rooted in Plautus' plays *c.* 200 B.C.) became Pagliaciaccio, who became Peppe Nappa, who became Pierrot.

As the principal characters evolved, many spin-off personalities emerged. A character's family tree can be traced, based on similarities of costume, mask, and character traits. Trivelino post-dates Arlecchino but claims to have been his father. Arlecchino, of course, became Harlequin when the character went to France.

Brighella has brothers in the person of Beltrame, Mezzetino, Flautino, and in Moliere's Scapin. Il Capitano's entourage includes Spavento, Giangurgolo, Rogantinok, and Scaramouche. Il Dottore became the model for all pretenders to wisdom, primarily in the fields of education, medicine, and law.

THE MASKS OF THE COMMEDIA DELL'ARTE

There is no way to know exactly what the commedia masks of the 1550s looked like. There are no leather masks of this period still in existence.

A variety of artist's renderings are shown on the next few pages, to portray the masks of the commedia dell'arte. They are from a wide assortment of sources, and they cover a time span from about 1550 to 1700.

Maurice Sand is the most famous of the commedia illustrators. His research was thorough and his drawings beautiful. His descriptions and engravings were printed in 1800, and mask makers since that time have relied heavily on his illustrations.

France and Italy have a few authentic leather masks in museums, but they are a precious few and from a period 150 years later.

This mask, from the Grand Opera Museum in Paris, is one of the oldest authentic leather masks still in existence. It is a zanni, obviously related to Arlecchino.

We also have the etchings of Jacques Callot (1592–1635) for whom the commedia was a favorite theme. He was prolific in his treatment of the subject.

Giuseppe Mitelli, Claude Gillot, Antoine Watteau, Carlo Lindstrom, and others also certainly capture the spirit of the commedia.

The statues illustrated on the following pages are from the villa of Montegaldella in Vicenza, Italy. A series of these life-sized commedia figures was done by Orazio Marimali in the 17th century to decorate the garden there. Time has taken its toll on these statues; a hand is missing here and a nose there, but the flavor of the work is retained.

The mask designs shown are the result of a heterogeneous blend of these sources.

Zanni

The long nosed, acrobatic, story-telling clown. The earliest of the commedia dell'arte characters worked alone and was known by the generic name "Zanni."

From an engraving by Jacques Callot

Arlecchino

Arlecchino is the simple, childlike, innocent clown, and faithful valet. He is simple, but no simpleton—he is not stupid. It's just that the logical things of this world escape him because he observes it through the eyes of a young child. If he sees an apple, and he is hungry, he will eat it—with no thought of ownership—and certainly no thought of stealing it. His needs are simple —food, staying out of trouble, and his love, Columbina. He remains always in love and always in trouble.

Arlecchino enjoys what he sees; for him, everything is a game. He does not think of the future and forgets what is out of sight. He acts first and then thinks, if he thinks at all.

From an engraving by Giuseppe Maria Mitelli

He has lived in a world of adults his whole life and is familiar with the way adults treat children —they hit. He is ever on the lookout for hits. Flinching is an accepted way with him. His move-ments are jerky and defensive. He travels in a zigzag skip as though fearful that lightning may strike him if he dares to dance in a straight line.

From an engraving by Maurice Sands

Somersaults and back flips are appropriate when he is happy, and he will take a rolling tumble backwards when his master slaps. Falling is as natural to Arlecchino as it is to a young child, and he picks himself up as unhurt and unashamed as a toddler.

The Mask

The earliest mask of Arlecchino (1550) consisted of a half-mask, full crown, and a chin strap. The mask was black, with a row of stiff whiskers extending from the ears to form a mustache. The nose was small, round, and slightly pug. A carbuncle grew from the forehead and the eye holes were small and perfectly round.

MASQUE AUTHENTIQUE DE ZANI. (CUIR ET CRIN. LES SOURCILS MANQUENT)
(Musée du grand Opéra á Paris.)

Later (1600) the masks became modifications of this early model. The facial hair is lost, but a sort of handlebar mustache (which might be read as cheekbones) is sculpted into the mask. The pug nose, carbuncle, and black color remain. The expression of a cat (or kitten) is sought, as an eye shape is sculpted into the features. When the round holes are punched into the mask for the actor's vision, they appear as pupils within the cat's eyes. The eyebrow is arched to convey a look of wide-eyed innocence. Some of the present-day mask makers in Italy try for a primitive animal quality in Arlecchino and are consciously aware of "cat" as they sculpt his mask.

The Costume

The early costume (1550) was white blouse, trousers, and close-fitting cap with a floppy brim. Soon (1600) patches and tatters were sewn to all parts of the fabric, to denote poverty. A belt was added to the jacket. Thrust in the belt was a slapstick which Arlecchino proudly wore as a sword. His hat was decorated with a rabbit's tail, as was the custom of the peasants of the time.

In another generation the patches became triangles. Then, at the end of the 17th century, the patches were the shape of diamonds, completely covering the costume; the breeches were form fitting. He had a cape, he was French, and his name was Harlequin.

Brighella

Brighella is the manipulating drifter from Bergamo. The character changed over the years, evolving from a likable, sly trickster in the 16th century to that of a bizarre, disturbing criminal in the 17th century, and then a hundred years later, back to the roguish knave.

He is a thief when it suits his purpose; the leather money bag he carries is rarely empty. That is a knife he has tucked in his belt; murder is not out of the question if it comes to that. He certainly has no desire for a slapstick. His audience accepts his evil as comic rascality, because it is broad and aimed at a common enemy—the wealthy. Brighella is a man with great charisma and no conscience. He will attempt anything, no matter how unscrupulous, if it is likely to bring him his desired results, and his success rate is very high. He has interest in money only as it will bring him pleasure. Once he has money in his pocket, all work ceases till he has enjoyed the last penny.

From an engraving by Stefano Della Bella

On the prowl he has the grace of a tiger; when cornered, the cunning of a rat; and he possesses the skill and agility of a monkey. He sings, plays the guitar, and knows how to dance. In the 18th century Brighella lost his lust for adventure and tended to keep his knife in its sheath.

The Mask

As the character of Brighella changed with the passage of time so did his mask. The earliest

It was dark brown. The nose was flatter, more blunted than that of Arlecchino. There was no carbuncle. The long sweeping cheek line more resembled a cheekbone than a mustache. The eye holes were cut large so the performer's eyes could be used expressively.

mask (1550) was not greatly different from that of Arlecchino.

From an engraving by Maurice Sands

Toward the end of the 16th century the color of the mask changed, as did the costume, to a shade of olive green. The widely published etchings of Maurice Sands show Brighella with a sinister eyebrow and with dark and deep set eyes. The nose is prominent and hooked. He wears a mustache made of real hair that is twirled at the ends, giving him an air of insolence.

The Costume

At first the costume consisted of the cap, loose white shirt, and baggy white trousers common to all comics. As the character matured, his jacket and trousers were tailored to become a servant's livery and were decorated with green frogs, braids, and chevrons. His accessories included a white mantle and a beret.

Pantalone

Pantalone is the old, miserly rake of Venice. Once a successful tradesman or merchant, he is now retired from active business. His body is pinched with age. His arthritic knees make it difficult for him to walk, but he is willing to attempt a shuffling run if the lady he is pursuing makes that action necessary. He may be a bachelor; if so he spends much time making a fool of himself with the young girls. Or he may be married, with a grown family. In that case he is trying to marry his daughter to a man of wealth, without providing her with a dowry.

Careful as he is with his purse, and suspicious as he is about those around him, he is easily duped out of his money by his wife, by his pretended lovers, by his children, and especially by his servants. He is the original "no respect" recipient. He is frequently accompanied by a servant, and the commedia dell'arte is full of examples of dialogues between this duo.

From an engraving by Jacques Callot

Part of Pantalone's tradition is that, in spite of his portrayed age, he is uncharacteristically athletic, and the most acrobatic member of the commedia troupe. His fury is accompanied by baffling outbreaks of agility. A ridiculous back fall is his reaction to bad news. He takes his pratfalls with all the vigor of youth and then immediately returns to a posture of old age and asthmatic panting.

The Mask

The half mask of Pantalone portrays age. The face is shallow, sunken, and bony. Its coloring is brown. His nose is pronounced and hooked, and his eyebrows are accentuated.

From an engraving by Maurice Sands

He has long, gray, windswept eyebrows. The color, shape, and texture of the hair on the mask matches that of the mustache and jutting beard on the actor's chin. Pantalone's profile is unique. Realizing this, the actor capitalizes on this position as often as is prudent during performance.

The Costume

In the mid 1500's Pantalone is pictured wearing tight-fitting red trousers. His jacket is short, buttoned in the front, is also tight fitting, and also red. His hat is brimless, close fitting, conical, typical of those worn by the doges of Venice. He shuffles around in slippers. Sometimes these are soft, yellow mules with open heels, but more likely they are Turkish slippers with the characteristic pointed toes. The robe is black (lined in red) with wide, elbow-length sleeves. Pantalone's belt supports both a money bag and a sheathed dagger. The dagger is almost never drawn, but is worn improperly in the front of his body, hanging between his legs for its comic effect. Some sketches show Pantalone wearing knee-length red stockings and trousers that are bloused at the knee.

Il Capitano

Il Capitano is the swaggering, cowardly, braggart soldier from Spain. In the beginning the Captain was, naturally enough, from Italy, and modeled after an early Roman prototype. He talks a much better fight than he is capable of. He finds pride in his fantasies concerning the men he has cut and carved and the widows he has made and the fair hearts he has slain. He is vain about his supposed good looks, and is convinced he can conquer any lady he chooses.

Spain dominated Italy under the rule of Charles V from 1520 to 1559. Commedia dell'arte performers found a perfect way to ridicule their oppressors — the captain became Spanish. His uniform took the colors and trimmings of the Spanish officers. The captain spoke with a nasal twang in a Castilian dialect, or a mixture of Spanish and Italian. The change of costume did not change his basic nature, however; for while strutting and boasting of his bravery, and rattling his sword, the sight of Arlecchino's slapstick still brought terror to his heart.

From an engraving by Maurice Sands

Should two captains happen to meet on the public square, you never saw such bravery. The rules of the battle were perfectly clear to both warriors. Neither had any reason to fear. The swords that each feared to draw in the presence of another man were drawn, crossed, flourished, and parried but never thrust as they maneuvered for position.

Cap. Mala Gamba. Cap. Bellauita .

88

From an engraving by Jacques Callot

The Mask

The first Captain's mask was flesh colored and had an enormously long nose reminiscent of that of the earlier zannis.

From an engraving by Maurice Sands

When the character began to mock the Spanish military the mask grew a heavy fake mustache and the long nose became more phallic. In the late 1500s the performer abandoned the use of the mask, preferring to use his own eyes and authentic long bristling mustache for expression, setting his face in a ferocious leer. One extant script has him wearing glasses so the ''terrific glare of his eyes may not put to shame the less ardent rays of the sun.''

The Costume

The earliest Captain wore the same white blouse and trousers that other comics wore. In addition, he wore a cape, a sword, and a wide-brimmed hat with long feathers. As the Spanish soldiers appeared on Italian soil, the costume became tight-fitting trousers and jacket with red and yellow stripes, a huge starched ruff, a plumed hat, garters or riding boots, and a dress sword with a fancy handle. Colored bands, ribbons, braids, and shiny buttons added some pomp to this ensemble.

Il Dottore

The Doctor is the pompous, blowhard academician from Bologna. He was born a learned man just as lesser mortals are born beautiful or ugly.

In the belief that wisdom commands respect, he buries men with his verbiage. He is the know-it-all bore with the wrong answer for all occasions.

He takes himself very seriously, meddling in everyone's business, forever advising, prescribing, and explaining. He sometimes carries an impressive book in one hand, referring to it as he lectures with his index finger. He is given to misquotations. He is equally at ease with his native tongue, an obscure foreign language, or gibberish.

The Doctor is obese and is therefore the least agile of the commedia characters. His round belly hangs over his belt. He sways as he walks with short steps, affecting a daintiness that simply is not his.

This pseudo-learned man shares some qualities with Pantalone: he is old, easily falls victim to the pranks of his servants, and while he is waging an unsuccessful amorous adventure with a young lady, it is likely his wife is making him a cuckold.

This ostentatious character began as a physician, but could be portrayed as a lawyer, astronomer, mathematician, or logician.

The Mask

The mask of the doctor is black, and covers only the forehead and nose. The single feature of the mask, the nose, is bulbous, but not so large as to cover the character's real mustache and rouged cheeks.

From an engraving by Maurice Sands

The Costume

In keeping with the dress of the real professors of the Bologna University in the 16th century, the costume of Il Dottore is black with a few white accents. He wears a black frock with a wide white collar and white cuffs. The academic gown falls below his knees, and is gathered with a belt at the waist. Black pants show beneath the gown and a black cape covers the doctor's shoulders. His shoes are black with heels and large buckles or bows. A black skullcap fits over the mask and covers the actor's hair. A wide-brimmed felt hat was introduced in 1653 to the costume by Augustin Lolli and has become a part of this character's tradition.

Pulcinella

Pulcinella is the cruel, selfish, humpbacked schizoid from Naples. Pulcinella was the direct descendant of two characters from the Roman theater, Bucco and Maccus. At times, he identified with one of these fathers, and at other times with the other. His character remained somewhat fluid, changing with the locale in which he performed and with the actor playing the role. Pulcinella became vastly popular in Naples in the early 17th century, and the audience had no trouble with the duality of personalities. On occasion, two Pulcinellas could appear on stage together; both were zannis and quite comfortable with the idea of playing a scene together. (In 1987, Mauriceo Scarparro did them one better, producing a theater piece set at a school for Pulcinellas, where at least nine Pulcinellas appeared on the stage simultaneously.)

In spite of the confusions of identity, these things could be said about Pulcinella in the early 1600's. He was self centered and self sufficient. He was quick, witty, and capable of biting irony. He was coarse, vulgar (even obscene), dishonest, and inclined to gluttony. Adept with a stick, he could use it as an instrument of persuasion to win his argument. He was sometimes pictured as having children, but was usually portrayed as an aging bachelor.

From an engraving by Carlo Lindstrom

You could be much more sure of Pulcinella's physical appearance than his character traits. A dorsal hump grew from his shoulder, and he sported a potbelly. As his character evolved, Pulcinella's hump grew larger. As the hump grew, the belly extended to set his carriage in balance.

From an engraving by Maurice Sands

The Mask

The mask was colored very dark brown or black. It had a worried, wrinkled brow, many warts and moles, and a prominent parrot beak of a nose that looked as if it would be at home on a hunchback.

As the mask matured, it took on a crudeness to match his cruelty and lack of refinement. Toward the end of the 17th century the face was rough textured with multiple blemishes and the nose (which now appeared to have been broken) gave the mask an asymmetrical quality.

From an engraving by Maurice Sands

The Costume

Pulcinella wore the loose white linen blouse that was in general use among the peasants. The long shift, which ran to almost mid-thigh, was belted at the waist and showed white trousers beneath. He wore a conical sugar-loaf hat. The costume had some mutations through the years, and in the various countries as the character traveled, but the loose white costume has come to be traditional with Pulcinella.

In time, Pulcinella had descendants of his own in the persons of Meo-Patacca, Cucurucu, and then later in England Jack Pudding and Punch from the puppet stage.

Cucurucu was a spin-off character who capitalized on the combination of hump, belly, and skinny legs to look like a chicken. He wore feathers in his hat and strutted and crowed like a rooster.

The Suitors

The suitors are youthful, sentimental, argumentative, scheming, and beautiful (or handsome).

Both the "lovers" (the gentlemen) and their "inamorata" (their beloved) are experts in the arts of courtship and are prolific writers of sonnets. They love, despair, they are suspicious and jealous. They part, are reconciled, and in the end they fly into each other's arms on their way toward the best possible marriage.

Orazio (1645)

From an engraving by Maurice Sands

There were usually two sets of lovers to keep the romantic interests occupied. The lovers could be children of the principal players or perhaps their maids and servants.

The lovers were called Flavio, Lelio, Leandro, Fabrizio, Ottavio, etc. The beloved was Isabella, Flaminia, Vittoria, Colombina, Camilla, or Lavinia. But whatever their names, their chief character trait is that of being in love.

The Mask and Costume

The greatest asset of the male lovers and their female counterparts was their comeliness, so neither wore a mask. The women were costumed in bonnets, skirts, and aprons, and both sexes wore the latest fashion of the period to which they belonged.

Colombine (1683)

From an engraving by Maurice Sands

MASK-MAKING WORKSHOP
IN PADUA, ITALY

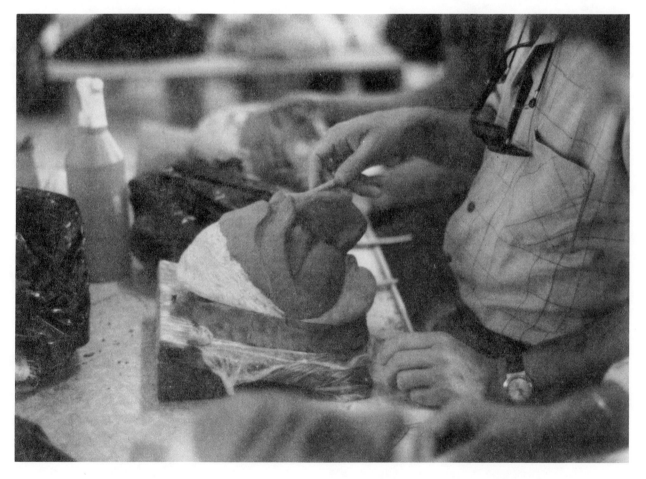

*Augusto Cabrera sculpting a mask for Pulcinella. The plaster life mask
beneath the clay is that of Augusto himself.*

In the summer of 1988, Professor Tom Wheatly of the UCLA theater department faculty gathered ten interested students to attend a leather mask-making workshop in Italy. Daniel Jue, who worked with me extensively as an undergraduate, was fortunate enough to be one of this group. The class, taught by master mask maker and sculptor Donato Sartori, met daily, seven hours a day for four weeks in a villa in Abono Terme, just outside Padua, Italy.

I visited this workshop as a guest of Mr. Sartori, staying with Prof. Wheatly, in one of the rooms in this centuries old villa. For the week of my stay, I was allowed full freedom to observe and photograph the classes in session, and to watch the craftsmen on Sartori's staff as they constructed masks (of Sartori's design) which had been commissioned. I attempted, with little success, to communicate with these craftsmen (both men and women). They spoke French and Italian, and I had only English, but I learned a great lesson in this experience: your questions will be answered if you keep your mouth shut and just watch—most of my ''whys'' were satisfied with patient observation.

Donato and his father, Amleto Sartori, developed techniques of leather mask making that must not be lost through disuse. Donato is committed to a plan of sharing his methods of interpreting and sculpting mask forms. Besides the recurring summer workshops at Il Centro Maschere e Strutture Gestuali, he has produced instructional video tapes and five books that I am aware of—three volumes in Italian, one in German, and one in English (see Bibliography on page 199).

THE ITALIAN WAY:
AN OVERVIEW OF LEATHER MASK MAKING

Dan Jue designed and constructed the mask in the following illustrations while attending Donato Sartori's workshop at Il Centro Maschere e Strutture Gestuali, in Abono Terme, Italy.

The old world tradition of leather mask making calls for six steps of mold preparation, culminating with at least eight more steps of tooling the leather over a wooden pattern. You are already familiar with most of the preliminary steps that lead up to carving the wood.

1. Plan the mask. Donato Sartori teaches that the mask, costume, gestures, and character are one, and they must not be separated. Study the character and his mental posture. Think about the character's likes, dislikes, and prejudices. Consider the motives that compel him to action. Then reflect on how these attitudes will affect the character's movements, his posture, and his facial expressions. Dan has chosen to portray a character of his own imaginings—an impoverished, homeless old man.

2. Sketch the expression. Make several sketches from several points of view.

3. Sculpt the mask in clay. This design is being formed from a fine grade of water-based clay. The sculpture may be built over a life mask of the performer; indeed this mask is being built over a life mask taken from Dan himself.

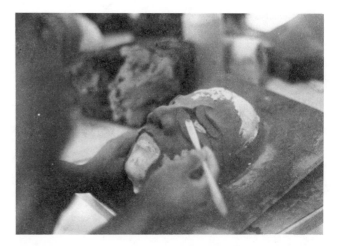

4. Make a plaster casting of the clay sculpture. The walls of this casting are thin. These were carefully held to a uniform thickness of about ½ inch.

5. Make a solid positive plaster casting from the negative mold. They used a waste mold tech-nique similar to the one explained in the section on Making a Positive Gypsum Cement Mold (page 79).

6. Carve the mask from a wooden block. The mask makers here used pine and carved the wood with a variety of chisels and gouges.

This is a precise, line-by-line replica of the plaster casting. The nose was chosen as a fixed reference. Dividers and calipers have been constantly in use, transferring the measurements from the plaster as the wood was carved.

When the carving was finished, Dan used a file and sandpaper to smooth the pine and make the wooden copy as like the plaster original as possible.

7. Nail the wetted leather to the wooden form. Nails should be driven in the underside of the mold, and into the eye sockets and the nostrils.

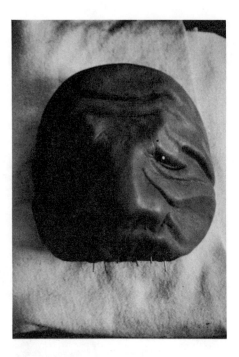

8. Press the leather in all depressions of the wooden mold. The leather was worked with fingers and a wooden tool to conform to the mold.

9. Force the leather to lie close to the wooden mold. At a precise moment in the leather's drying, the leather can be driven to the wood surface by pecking at it with the pointed end of a horn hammer.

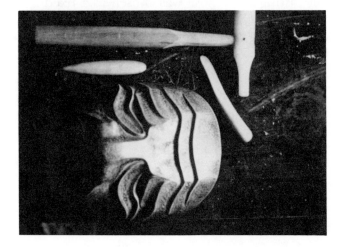

10. Further compress the leather with the flat surface of a hammer made of plastic or wood. This pounding eliminates the pit holes left by the sharp pointed horn.

11. Polish the formed leather with a hardwood stick.

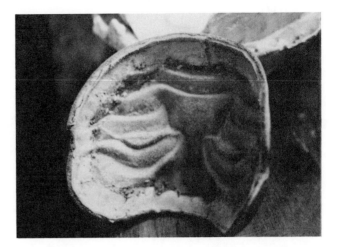

12. Remove the nails, and finish the perimeter and interior of the mask.

13. Seal the interior of the mask with varnish.

14. Color the exterior of the mask with dyes.

MAKING A MASK
IN LEATHER

Signor Universo putting the finishing touches on this mask of Arlecchino.
It is part of a set of masks that were commissioned from the studio.

Leather is always formed over a hard positive shape. Most (but not all) of the design possibilities of the mask are in the creation (or selection) of this solid pattern. The form itself can be of any firm material. The Italian mask makers traditionally carve their molds from wood. This book recommends and demonstrates techniques of making the mold from a hard gypsum cement.

LEATHER MASK CHARACTERISTICS

Leather has most of the desirable qualities you would want to find in a mask-making material. It is lightweight; the surface is flexible and smooth; and it is very comfortable. Perspiration is never troublesome, as it is absorbed into the surface of the leather. The leather is described by some performers as being a "second skin."

An uncared-for mask made of leather can have a life approximating that of an old shoe—leather is very durable. If, however, you do care for it—packing it so it doesn't get crushed, keeping it from drying out, and protecting it from the deteriorating effects of ultraviolet light—it will last for many years more. The mask does not worsen through use in performance.

A piece of leather large enough to build a normal half mask should not cost more than $10.00.

The good qualities of leather make up for its one shortcoming. Leather mask making can be a very time consuming activity. The positive mask mold takes a little longer to prepare, and then, when it's time to form the leather, you cannot afford to be impatient.

TANNING

Once an animal skin goes through a tanning process it becomes leather. Tanning is an irreversible process which chemically neutralizes the tissues, fat, blood vessels, and nerves of the hide. All of the protein of the skin forms a chemical bond with the ingredients of the tanning solution. Leather has many of the properties and characteristics of its previous self, but chemically it is a new substance. An animal skin is subject to decay and eventual decomposition, but tanned leather has great permanency.

Mask makers of the past have used the skins of pigs, goats, deer, and cattle. Early European mask makers, however, worked out the techniques of shaping cowhide, and it has become the exclusive standard in Western cultures.

Cowhide can be cured into leather in three distinctly different processes. Chamois cloths are oil tanned. Shoes and most leather used for clothing are tanned with a process involving minerals (chrome tanning). Leather used for making belts, wallets, and other crafts projects is tanned with organic materials (vegetable tannin —derived from trees and shrubs). Chrome-tanned leather is much too stable to be shaped into a mask. On the other hand, vegetable-tanned leather can be sculpted and shaped under the influence of water and tooling. The techniques of shaping leather described in this section are only possible with a skin that has been cured with vegetable tannin. This leather is readily available from a tannery or leather-crafts store.

PREPARING THE MOLD

I want to quarrel with the idea that carving the mask form in wood is absolutely necessary. Carving the wooden mold is time consuming and hard work (and more important perhaps—I am not talented at wood carving). After experiencing my first project of carving a mask form of wood, I began to search for a faster, easier, and better(?) way.

It is argued that 1) the wooden form is a necessary cushioning agent during the hammering process; 2) the wooden form is helpful in absorbing water from the leather thus hastening the drying; and 3) you need a tacking surface to secure the leather to the mold during the forming.

On the surface, these three arguments seem compelling. However, it is my experience that the first two points—cushioning and absorption—are not really valid. Continued pounding on a Hydrocal mold may eventually break it down, but you can get 10 to 12 leather masks from one mold. A wooden mold shows signs of wear after about 20 leather reproductions are made. The wooden form is always varnished, making it moisture resistant, and a Hydrocal mold is just as absorbent as varnished wood.

A gypsum cement form would make a valid leather-shaping mold if we could just tack the leather to the backside of the mold.

Providing a Tacking Surface to a Cement Mold

I propose that we make the front of the mold from gypsum cement, then bond a softer material, one that has characteristics of wood, to the backside of the mold. The hard, durable surface of the cement receives and preserves the features of the mask form, and the soft surface of the backside receives the tacks. We will do this in two different ways. 1) Modify a mold you have in stock, scooping out a portion of the mold and filling the depression with wood putty; and 2) sculpting a new character mask, embedding a block of wood in the backside of the mold.

Modifying a Stock Mold

This positive gypsum cement mold was originally used to produce a mask made of Celastic. It can be altered to be suitable for shaping leather by treating the surface on the rear with wood putty.

When making a leather mask, you must fold the leather to the rear of the mold, at the precise edge of the mask. The form and the shape of this border, therefore, must be determined at the outset.

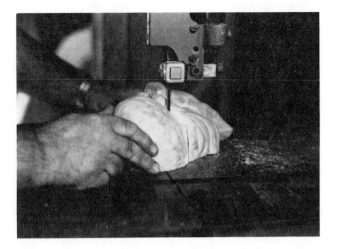

Design and trace the outside shape of the mask. The cheeks and lower jaw, which are not a part of the mask, will be removed by carefully cutting the mold on this line with a band saw. When the lower jaw is removed, the leather can be folded to the back along the upper lip line as planned.

Treat the mold with a disk sander, removing ¾ inch concave scoops in the lower part of the mold and in its backside.

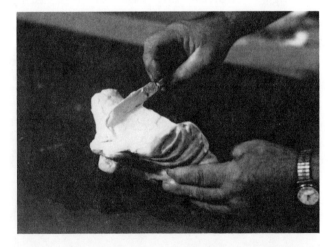

Use a heavy application of wood putty to fill the spaces removed with the saw and sander. When

the putty cures, you can secure the leather to the mold with small tacks.

Preparing a Mold from a New Sculpture

If you are starting to sculpt and build a new character mask, you can design the mold to have the desired contours. It can even be built to accommodate a backing made of real wood.

The illustrations show two molds under construction. The clay model on the left is a neutral half mask, the one on the right is the commedia dell'arte character Arlecchino.

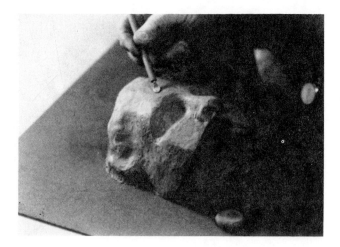

Sculpt the mask form from modeling clay as you have done in the former mask-making projects. Do not concern yourself with the problems of the back of the mold yet. You cannot carve the scoops into the model at this stage of the process. We deal with the scooped depressions by modifying the negative mold, as shown on the next page.

Carefully plan the edges of the masks. The perimeter of the neutral mask has been defined in the clay sculpture. The border of Arlecchino has been precisely outlined with a wall of clay. Either of these mold-making techniques is acceptable.

Finish the clay sculpture by smoothing the surface of the form with your fingers and a light coating of petroleum jelly. Mix a batch of casting plaster and make a negative casting.

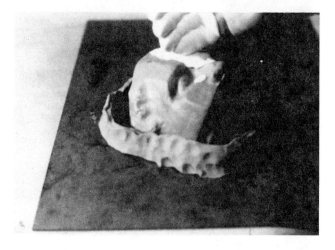

Make an impression coating. Add plaster till the casting is about ½ inch thick.

When the plaster has cured, remove the clay sculpture, and clean up the scrap bits of clay from the interior of the negative mold. All the steps to this point should be very familiar to you; they are not different from the techniques outlined earlier in the section on Making a Negative Mold (page 60).

You have all the features of the mask and the size and shape of its boundaries in negative form. Now is the time to make the modifications so the mold can receive tacks. Before the positive Hydrocal form is poured, add a wedge of modeling clay to the negative mold in any place that you wish to drive tacks. When the positive form is cast, and these tapering wads of clay are removed, they leave a concave void that can be filled with putty.

On the neutral half mask, we shaped the clay from the forehead line, making a convex wall that tapered toward the center of the mold. This wall should be at least ¾ inch thick at its thickest part. A thinner wall will not provide a good bed of putty in the finished mold and the tacks may not hold fast.

We made the same kind of clay wall in the lower part of the mask, beginning the convex wedge precisely along the jaw line and tapering it inward toward the center of the mold.

The rear of the mold can be filled with an actual block of wood. Cut a piece of pine that form-fits the opening and mount some bolts firmly to the block.

When the mold is filled with Hydrocal and the block is pressed into the wet cement, the bolts become bonded firmly in place. The wooden block should be cut about ¾ inch smaller than the actual opening so it does not interfere with the true shape or the strength of the walls of the negative mold.

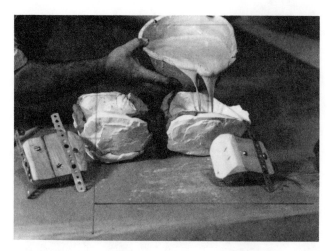

Fill the mold so the casting material rises up flush to the top, completely surrounding the block of wood.

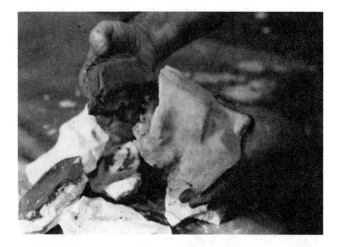

Break away the plaster negative mold (consistent with the waste mold procedure) and remove the wedge of modeling clay. The convex depressions in the positive mold are immediately obvious.

Rebuild these voids by filling them with a water putty that has the consistency of wood when it is cured. Durham's Rock Hard Water Putty is one such product.

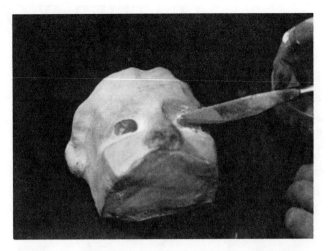

The eyes of the finished mask will be cut open, so the leather can be tacked in these places without leaving flaws. Prepare the area on the mold by drilling ¾ inch holes into the eye sockets, and again, patch the holes with putty.

LEATHER-WORKING TOOLS

A few of the tools required for shaping leather are special and must be purchased at a leather-crafts store. Two of the most important tools are so special you will have to make them yourself. Leather-working tools are not new; they are at least a hundred years old, being used by farmers and horsemen to make and repair harnesses. The major tools have not changed in this time; the 1902 Sears Catalogue has pictures of a skiver, an edger, and a strip-cutting gauge that look very contemporary.

Tools for making masks must be made of a material that does not discolor the leather. Wet leather stains when it is brought in contact with iron and steel, so the tools must be made of wood, bone, horn, plastic, or stainless steel. The items you find in a leather crafts store will most likely be made of stainless steel.

Shown here are a leather punch, a skiver, an edger, a rivet set, an edge slicker, a strip-cutting gauge, and a mallet. Each tool will be fully explained and demonstrated as it is used on the following pages. Don't run out and buy all of these tools right away. You will not have an immediate need for most of them.

You cannot buy the two basic tools that are used to shape leather. You must make them for yourself.

Sticketta

The first tool is a wooden blade used for shaping and polishing the leather. I don't know a good name for this tool; I have heard it referred to here in the United States as a "sculptor's thumb," a good descriptive term but an awkward name. The Italians call it a "sticketta." Although the tool has some of the appearance of a knife blade it must have no really sharp edges. The blade must be made of a hard wood with very tight, even grain. In Italy they use "boxwood," but this tree is not grown in the U.S. and its wood is considered to be exotic here. The hardwood specialist at the lumber yard tells us it is somewhat like maple.

You should have no trouble finding a piece of hardwood to build yourself a "sticketta." An old baseball bat is probably made of hickory or walnut. I don't know what the golf club here is made of, but this putter is about the size of a blade. The pool cue is made of ash. The table leg is made of oak or mahogany.

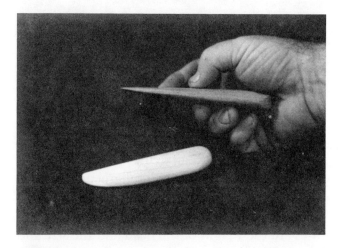

You might find any or all of these items at a thrift shop. A batting cage should have a broken baseball bat. A pool hall should have a ready supply of broken cue sticks, and once they're broken you can't use them to shoot pool any more.

The shaping blade is about 4½″ long and ⅞″ wide. The top edge is even duller than the one you see facing you in the photo. Remember, this stick is for shaping the leather, not cutting it. Sketch the shape on a small piece of hardwood and rough cut it on a band saw. Refine the shape by working it on a disk sander. Then shape and smooth the blade with sandpaper. There must be *no* rough edges remaining on the wooden stick. Any coarse, abrasive spot will scratch the leather and continued rubbing will scuff a flaw in the surface. Use a very fine grit (400) sandpaper for the final smoothing of your stick.

Finally, your wooden blades should be soaked in linseed oil for about a week. It's a good idea to recondition the stick occasionally, as you use it, by rubbing it with a fresh application of linseed oil.

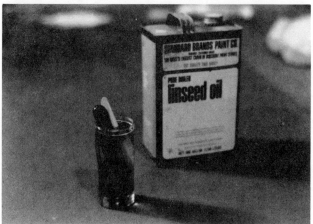

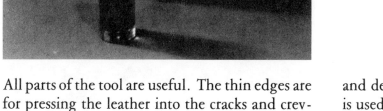

All parts of the tool are useful. The thin edges are for pressing the leather into the cracks and crevices of the mold. The butt end (which is shaped much like a thumb) is effective in shaping the eyes and deep depressions; the flat edge of the blade is used for forming sharp-edged features and for polishing the leather in the final stage of its forming. This is a simple but very necessary tool.

Cow Horn Hammer

You may think this next instrument is somewhat quaint, but be assured it is also a very practical tool. You need a sharp-nosed hammer for pecking at the leather. The hammer compacts the

leather, stretching it in some places, crowding it together in others, but always persuading it to lie close to the mold.

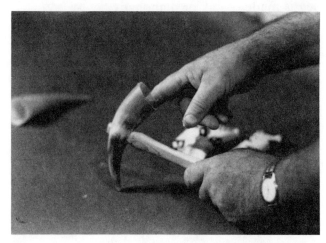

The hammer head is a steer's horn. The handle is a replacement part for a tack hammer. Drill holes through both sides of the horn, and enlarge them to an oval shape with a round wood file to accept the handle. This should be a tight fit.

Slip the handle in place. Bond the handle to the head by packing the hollow horn with a wad of two part, hand workable epoxy putty.

Examine the point on the horn. Sand the tip with 400 grit sandpaper to make it as smooth as possible and to dull it if that seems necessary. You will be able to make this judgment when you begin to use the hammer.

I have no doubt that this horn hammer could be made of hardwood or acrylic. The important features are the weight of the head and the size and shape of the tip. In Italy, however, they use a horn.

BASIC LEATHER FORMING

Selecting the Leather

Selecting the right piece of leather is of paramount importance. Obtain an appropriate size piece of vegetable-tanned leather from a leather store or tannery. Ask for cowhide belly that has been cured with vegetable tannins. The leather which has been cut from the belly is very different from a piece cut from the side or the shoulder. Craftsmen who tool and stamp their leather into belts, watchbands, and sandals prefer the tougher, thicker leather found on the shoulder and back of the animal. Wallets, handbags, and garments are thinner and most likely cut from the sides of the hide. The portion of leather taken from the cow's underbelly is usually shunned by the leather hobbyist because it is soft, pliable,

and scarred with stretch marks and flaws.

The belly works best for mask making because it is malleable, supple, soft. It willingly responds to the efforts of pressing, compressing, stretching, and shaping. You must, however, select your leather carefully to avoid the major flaws.

The belly is typically cut away from the main hide at the tannery and is sold separately. It is available as a rather long, narrow strip. You will have little trouble in finding a piece of flawless belly if you are making a half mask. You may have to make a friend at the tannery, however, to select a perfect piece of belly for a larger leather casting.

Preparations

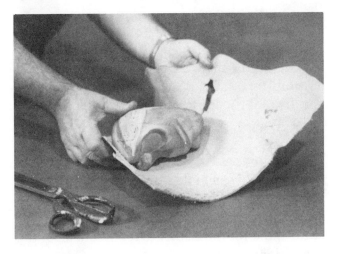

Wrap your mold in the strip of belly to determine the size of leather you will need. As you make this decision, be sure you allow plenty of fullness. The leather must be full enough to reach into the depressions in the face of the mask form.

Look for flaws in the leather. Adjust the position of the mold so any imperfection falls into an area that will be removed as the mask is cut to size.

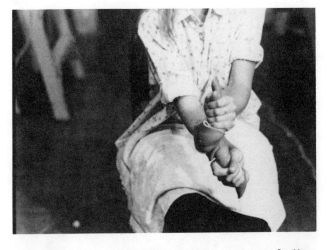

Submerge the leather in very hot water and allow it to soak for about 10 minutes—till it becomes completely saturated. Wring, twist, and rub it vigorously to soften the fibers. Knead it with some of the same intensity that an Eskimo woman might use in chewing reindeer skins to soften them.

[145]

When you begin to make a leather mask allow yourself a sufficient block of time so you can finish the basic shaping of the leather in one sitting. In the winter this may be as long as 6 to 7 hours. In the summer when the leather dries much faster, the job may be finished in almost half the time. The weight of the leather is another big factor in drying time. Thick leather acts as a sponge and dries slowly. Much of the computed time listed above will be spent waiting for the leather to get to the correct degree of dampness. But do not plan to begin the shaping today and finish it tomorrow.

Most of the work will be done with the mask in your lap as you sit in a straight-backed chair. A standard 30 inch table is just too high. A work bench about 26 inches high might be helpful, but working in the lap is very comfortable. Lay a towel over your legs to absorb moisture and keep your clothes clean.

Tacking the Leather

Press the leather into all of the depressions of the form before you tack it. Again we stress that you leave plenty of freedom for the leather to be molded into the concave portions of the pattern.

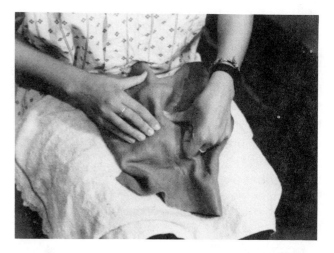

Common carpet tacks can be used to fasten the leather to the mold. These tacks are made of iron and will certainly blacken the leather they come in contact with, but the tacking surface will be cut away as the mask is finished, so there is really no problem. Tacks made of copper or brass do not discolor the leather in any way.

Tack the midpoint of all four sides of the leather to the back of the mold. Begin at the midpoints and work toward the corners. Check again to make sure there is sufficient fullness on the front of the mold for the leather to reach into all of the depressions.

Folds of surplus leather are likely to appear as you tack the leather around to the back of the mold. Do not allow this excess to cause you any despair!

Make every attempt to distribute the excess evenly around the form. Then, use a mat knife to cut V-shaped wedges to relieve this fullness. The point of the "V" should begin very close to the facial features of the mask and extend back as far as necessary to find a tacking surface. Clip away surplus leather that extends beyond the tack line. This extra leather will never be needed; all it does is create a lot of unwanted tensions.

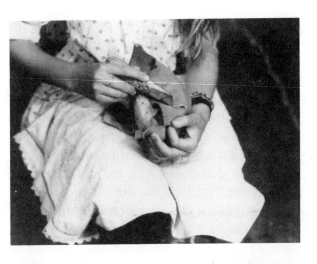

Continue to tack and remove surplus till the leather lies smoothly around the circumference of the backside. Make as many V-shaped wedges as you need—you cannot have too many.

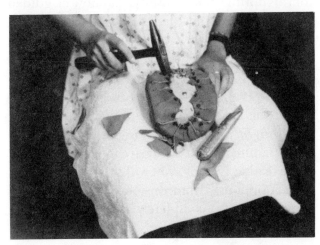

When leather is saturated with water it has its greatest elasticity. You can stretch it, forcing it into depressions, but it also tends to withdraw from these places, responding to the natural tensions of the leather when the pressure is released.

Pressing a Shape in the Leather
Begin immediately to rub the wet leather with the hardwood sticketta. Rub, press, and coax the leather into its new shape. As you rub the leather with your tool, keep the heaviest strokes running toward a low place rather than away from it. Urge the leather with your tool to fall into these depressions.

If you find it helpful, tack the leather into the deep depressions of the mask—the eyes and nostril holes. These parts will be cut away and the tack holes will not show when the mask is finished. At this point in your work, all of the features that were designed into the mask should be clear and distinct.

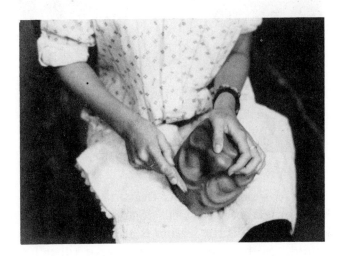

While you have been working on the mask the mold has been soaking some of the moisture away and the leather is beginning to dry out. That's good. It's necessary! You have been working for about one hour, and under normal circumstances the leather is too wet to carry the work any further. You may want to take a break. Don't be gone much longer than an hour, though.

The final shaping of leather should be done when it is almost dry. It is a little harder to make the leather move at this stage of minimum dampness, but it stays where you put it. Only experience will tell you how wet the leather should be for this optimum workability. For now be guided by the color of the leather. Dry leather is tan, wet leather is brown. As the color begins to turn light again, it is ready to be treated with the horn

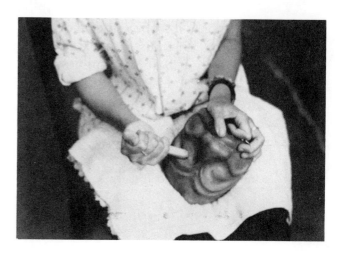

hammer. Beating on wet leather with the horn hammer is a waste of time and the repeated blows begin to pulverize the leather.

Working Leather with the Horn Hammer

When the leather is almost dry (that is to say it is still *slightly* damp) begin to peck at it with the horn hammer. You will have no more breaks. If the leather is ready, you will probably be working continuously from this point till the mask is completely dry, completely shaped, and has a shiny polish on its surface.

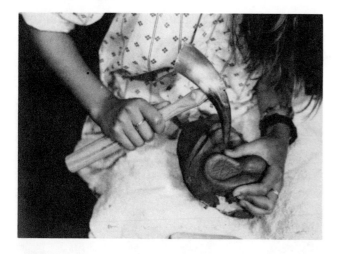

Each blow of the hammer treats the minute portion of leather it contacts, forcing it to conform to the mold. If the leather is bridging across the mold, the hammer point stretches it till it lies

Allow me to give you one more clue as to when the leather has attained this elusive optimum dampness—when you peck at the leather each blow will drive the moisture along, and if you look very closely you will be able to see it. The center of the dimple becomes light tan and the ridges of the pit go light brown.

Work on the mask, one plane at a time. The hammer will dimple the leather but should not break the surface of the grain. If you see that the hammer is breaking the skin, it is too dry (not likely), or the hammer is too sharp and the tip should be dulled with a file and smoothed with fine grit (400) sandpaper. Place the dimples as close together as you can make them. Overlap them if necessary, but attempt to lay in an irregular pattern that is all-encompassing. The effect of the hammer is twofold—it shapes the leather and compacts it, reducing the thickness by almost 1/3.

close. If there is a little fullness, the hammer blow compresses the leather till it hugs the surface of the mold.

Working the Leather with the Sticketta

As soon as you have finished dimpling one area of the mask, begin to work with the sticketta (the wooden blade). Rub the leather vigorously with the heavy end of the stick, smoothing out all evidence of the dimples you just made with the hammer. Your goal is to compress the ridges around the little pits to conform to the bottom of the pit itself, and to make the surface of the leather smooth again.

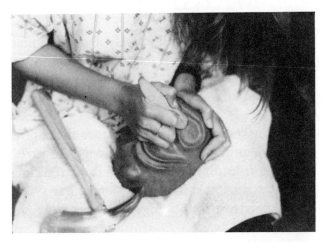

Select another plane on the mask, and begin again with the horn hammer. Work in an organized manner, one section at a time.

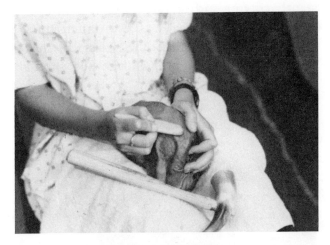

Again rub out all traces of the hammer blows with the wooden stick.

Polishing the Mask

When you have finished hammering and rubbing all of the features of the mask it will probably be almost dry. The final step in this stage of the operation is to polish the entire surface of the mask with the flat edge of the blade. Your purpose now is to search out and eliminate any remaining unevenness in the surface of the mask, and to polish the leather to a smooth gloss.

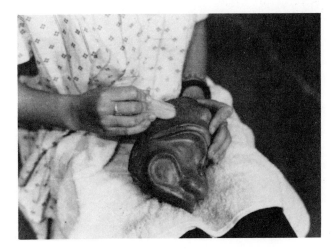

MAKING SHARP-ANGLED FEATURES

I asked Donato Sartori about the sharply defined features that distinguish the masks crafted in his studio. He gave me a short lesson on rounds *vs.* planes and why he strives for strongly faceted edges.

He picked up a coffee cup from the dinner table. ''I am suspicious of round-edged features, they are misleading,'' he said. (In thinking about this I am sure the translator should have said, ''I do not trust round-edged features, they are misleading.'')

Holding the cup high, he said ''The constantly curving surface catches light poorly, and from a distance it reads as two-dimensional.'' He then picked up a six-sided glass salt shaker and held it to the light. ''Notice how the flat-tened plane catches the light.''

He pointed to the salt shaker. ''These planes that fall in shadow are also well defined. When the shaker is viewed from a distance, the eye blends the flattened areas together, and the shaker is perceived as three-dimensional. It is round.''

He continued, ''This is true of the features of a face also; the actor knows this and frequently uses makeup to draw his features to appear sharply sculptured. A mask designed with many rounds tends to flatten out and lose its dimensional effect. But if you will flatten the edges of the features, the quality of your sculpture gains strength. When you isolate the planes, you are able to take full advantage of your stage lights.''

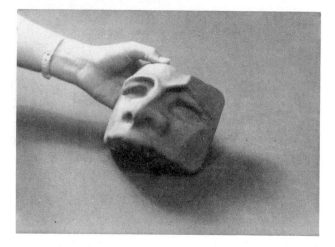

With this lesson still in our minds, let's work on the features of this mask of Brighella. It was sculpted with clearly defined features, but these will be delineated even more as the leather is worked. The leather in this photo has been wetted, tacked, and rubbed to conform to the mold, with fingers and a wooden tool.

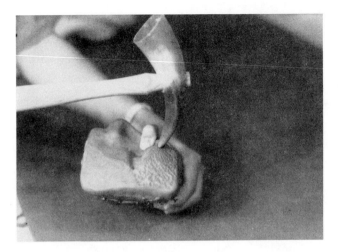

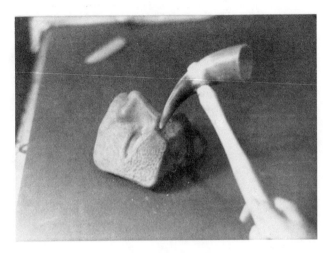

When you get to the hammering stage, peck at the leather, working one area at a time. Dimple the leather right up to the edge, but be careful *not* to put *any* blows of the hammer directly on the edge you are trying to define. Rotate the mask if it is necessary. Turn your tool if that helps you work right up to the edge. Never touch the edge itself with blows from the hammer.

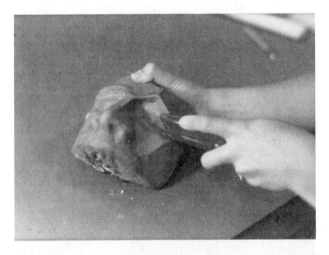

Polish the dimples till they are smooth, but keep the wooden stick flat to the plane you are working. Continually keep your stick parallel to the plane you are polishing or you will flatten the corner you are attempting to make sharp.

It sometimes helps to cut a slit in the eye of the mask to give the leather a little more freedom to fall in the deepest recesses of the mold. If you are careful with the placement of this cut it will not show when the eye is opened.

Vigorously rub the dimpled surface with your stick, polishing away all of the flaws made by the pointed hammer. Finally the leather will be smooth, dry, and finished.

This technique of working the edges of individual planes compresses the leather everywhere except on the specific corner you want to make sharp. On this corner the leather is a little bit puffy, and your stick simply shapes the fullness into a sharp edge.

Skiving

A skiving tool uses a standard injector-type razor blade, but it has nothing to do with the removal of hair. The skiver reaches deep into the leather and reduces its thickness, working on leather much as the carpenter's plane works on wood.

Your local leather-crafts store will have a variety of styles of skiving tools. The blade is cheap, easy to change, and should be replaced as often as necessary to keep the tool sharp.

There are at least three reasons you would want to use this tool: 1) to remove some unwanted coarseness missed by the tanner; 2) to reduce the thickness of the leather; and 3) to obtain skiving strips. You will see these skiving strips are very useful in finishing the interior of the mask and in making splices.

On some sections of belly, the flesh side of the leather is rough, granular, unrefined, and perhaps even spongy or slimy. Drawing the skive across a section of wet leather removes some of this coarseness.

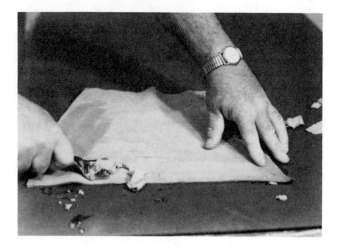

Drawing the skive repeatedly over a section of leather (wet or dry) effectively reduces its thickness. If you reduce the thickness of the leather that falls on intricate features of the mask, it makes them easier to work. This is not such a problem when you are working with belly, but we will speak more on this in the last section when we demonstrate how to shape larger pieces of side and shoulder.

Save the longer shavings that you obtain from these operations. The skiving strips are very useful. You may even have to make some of the strips from a piece of scrap leather just because you need them for the operations described on the next few pages.

MAKING A SPLICE IN LEATHER

I think you will agree that leather is somewhat marvelous in its willingness to conform to the shape of a positive mold. There is a limit, however, as to how far even a piece of belly will stretch. Sometimes you must make a splice in the leather in order for it to comply with the demands of an exaggerated shape.

The nose of this zanni is a case in point.

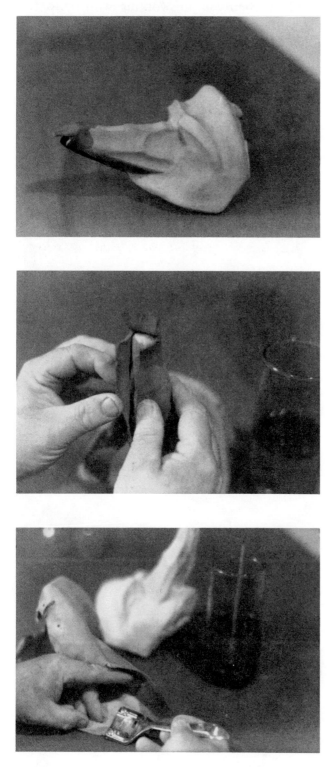

You simply *must* make a splice on the underside of the nose. Trim the leather on the underside of the nose so it has a ¼ inch flap that can overlap onto itself. Make this cut as a final step in shaping the leather.

The leather at the tip of the nose needs to be fashioned into a flap that can fold down, improving the appearance of the end. Trim the leather on the end so it neatly covers the tip of the nose when it is folded down. If necessary, wet the small portion of leather that you are working again. You can wet a small controlled area of the mask with a sponge, a cotton swab, or a paintbrush.

Remove the leather mask from its mold and spread it open on your work bench. This will no doubt cause a major distortion in your mask. Regrettable perhaps, but it is necessary and only temporary. You must fold the mask open in order to skive the leather along each edge of the splice. Shave a bevel along a ¼ inch strip of each edge of the overlap. The lower portion will be cut on the grain side (hair side), the upper portion that makes the flap should be cut on the flesh side. When these tapered edges are glued, they will fit together in such a manner that the splice will have a uniform thickness.

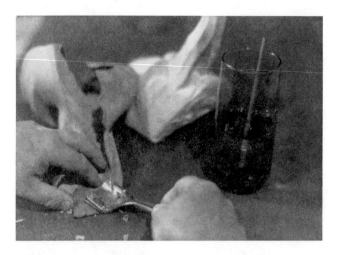

Skive the tab at the end of the nose till it is paper thin. The main part of the tab should be about the thickness of card stock, and the edges should taper to the thickness of typing paper.

If you are not very careful, you will cut unwanted holes in the leather, but if you have a sharp blade and work slowly and carefully the cut is possible.

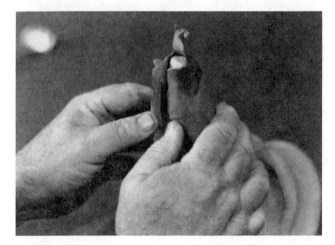

Reassemble the mask onto the mold and reshape the distortions by pressing the leather to the form with your hands. Close the flaps and see if the joint overlaps as it should. If the joint is not perfect, remove the mask and shave and trim it till it is.

The leather should still be moist enough to shape these thin flaps to lie down evenly. If not, brush on a little more water and use the wooden blade to force the edges flat.

The leather must be dry in order to glue it. If you are patient you can simply wait. The thin skived edges will dry quickly. If you are in a hurry, you can force dry the joints by gently blowing on the leather with a hair dryer.

Glue the flaps shut with a good contact cement. "Barge" rubber cement is made especially for use on leather, and is widely used by those who make and repair shoes.

Coat both parts of the joint, let the cement air dry for 10 minutes, then press the parts together. Vigorously rub the joint onto the hard surface of the mold to assure good contact between the glued parts.

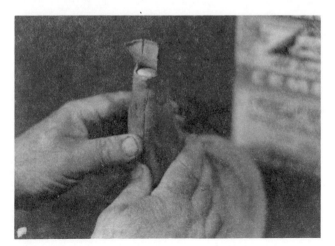

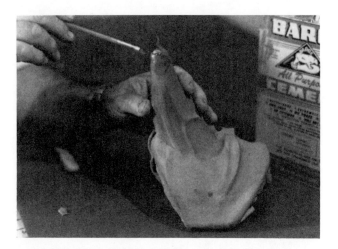

Trim the end flap till it is a perfect fit and glue it in the same way.

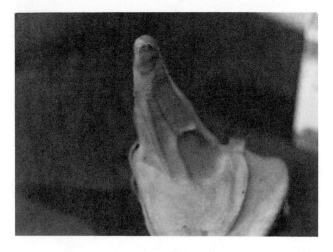

The Zanni and Il Capitano are two commedia masks that have traditionally sported elongated noses. The finished splices in the noses of these characters are almost imperceptible, even at close range, when they have each received a coating of dye and polish.

FINISHING THE PERIMETER OF THE MASK

The perimeter of the mask can be treated in two ways: by embedding a wire in its edge to stiffen it, or by just trimming away the surplus with a razor knife. The former method requires much more time but it raises the quality of the mask in both its appearance and in its life expectancy. If you are interested in selling your work, the stiffened edge can just about double the value of the mask.

Making and Trimming the Tabs

Remove all of the tacks. Each of these iron tacks has left a black stain in the leather, but the blemish does not matter because it will be cut away.

Trim away the surplus leather. As you trim, you will be making a series of tabs that extend about ¾ inch past the rim of the mask.

As we continue the construction of the mask of Arlecchino and carry it to its completion, we will show how to implant the wire. Trimming and treating a raw cut edge will be demonstrated in the section on Other Leather-working Techniques (page 179).

This mask has set for one day and is completely dry.

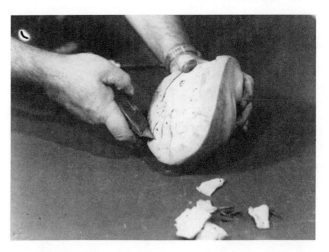

These tabs will fold into the inside of the mask, holding the stiffening wire in place (and hiding it). The tabs must be shaved paper thin to make the fold without substantially increasing the thickness of the border.

Use a *sharp* chisel to shave the tabs till they are literally thin as paper. Turn the chisel around so you are almost using it backwards. Although you are pulling the point of the chisel toward your body it is safe if you don't use your arm muscles to draw the blade. Use the controlled action of your wrist to draw the cutting edge into the soft leather.

Do not remove the leather from the Hydrocal form. The backside of the mold gives a good hard surface to support the leather as it is shaved.

Now you can remove the leather from the mold and test the ability of the tab to make a tight fold as it rolls back onto the interior of the mask. Is it thin enough? Or does it need some more attention? Very likely the part lying right next to the border is still too thick.

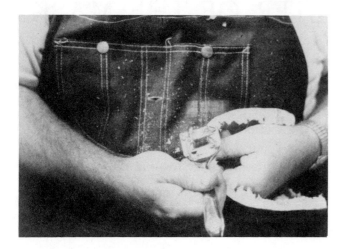

Hold the roll with one hand and draw a *sharp* razor blade (or a skiving tool with a *sharp* blade) across the thick place to reduce its bulk.

Wetting and Shaping the Tabs
Wet the border of the mask so you can press the flap tightly closed. Use a brush to control the water. The leather is so thin it takes very little water to saturate the edge. Be careful not to drip any water on the surface of your finished mask. The water will leave a water stain if you are not careful.

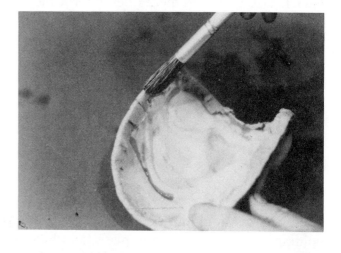

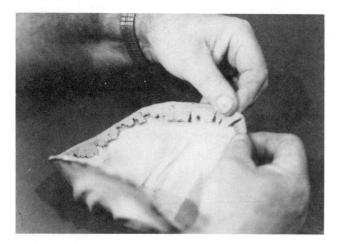

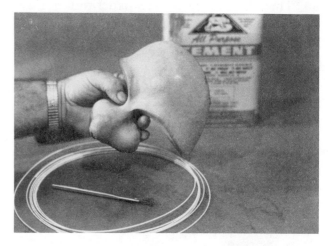

Use your fingers and your stick to close the flap and flatten it. Set the mask aside till the edge dries. The paper thin edge will dry in a few minutes. Use the time to get your glue and cut some wire for the next step. (Use a hair dryer to force dry the border if you are impatient.)

We introduce the mask of Il Dottore here because he has a special need of extra strength at the bridge of his nose. A wire stiffener is very helpful in keeping his nose from warping.

Inserting and Gluing the Wire

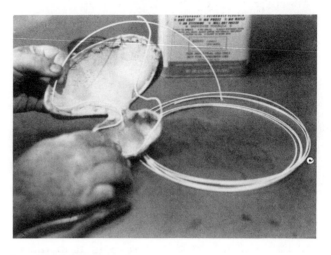

Use millinery wire. This wire is soft enough to bend into shape with your fingers, yet strong enough to retain the required shape. It is wrapped with cotton thread and reacts very well to the glue involved in the process.

Bend a general shape to the wire and cut a piece long enough to fit around the perimeter of the mask.

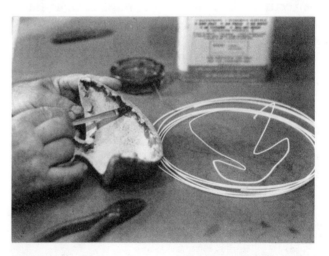

Use a good contact cement to glue leather. Barge cement is one glue that can be recommended. Use an expendable brush to apply the glue. Pry the tabs open and coat both surfaces that are going to be pressed together. Use an ample amount of glue. Don't be stingy, but at the same time don't get sloppy. *Do not allow any of the glue to get on the front of the mask.* Coating the wire is not necessary — it will pick up plenty of cement from the surface of the leather as it is fitted into place.

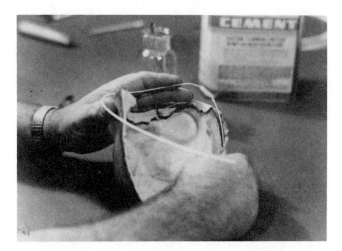

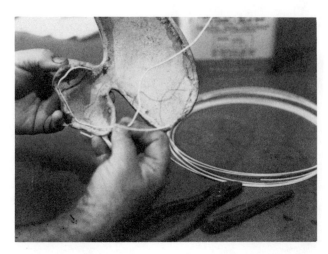

Fit the wire into one edge of the mask and press the paper-thin tabs over it to hold it in place. Hold the tab closed for a few minutes till the cement holds firmly. With one section of the wire thus held imprisoned in the edge flaps, it is easy to bend the next section of wire to conform perfectly to the border of the mask's edge. Bend the wire at the corner (use small pliers if neces-

sary), slip another section of wire into place, fold the tabs closed, and hold them shut till the wire is secure. Continue around the entire border of the mask. If you used an ample amount of glue on the first coating there should be no question of needing any more. Surfaces that have been well glued remain tacky and workable for at least 30 minutes.

Rub the tabs with your fingers and your sticketta. Press the sharpest edge of the stick alongside the wire and force it to the corner of the roll. Rub the joint to force the leather flap into the closest possible contact with the interior of the mask.

Lining the Border with Skived Leather
There is one more step required, if you want to put a fine finish on the interior of your mask. Glue thin leather strips to the border of the mask to provide a continuous smooth surface that covers

the wire and tabs.

You will need several of the strips of the very thin leather shown being cut on page 152 where Skiving was demonstrated.

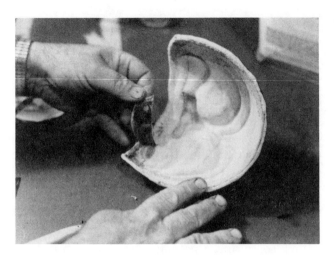

Select a strip of skived leather about ¾ inch wide and long enough to cover a long part of the contour of the border without buckling. Coat the strip and a band along the border of the mask with glue. Allow them to dry long enough to get tacky, and press the skived strip in place. It should come right up to the edge of the mask. The rim must be smooth, continuous, and comfortable where it comes in contact with the face of the performer.

SEALING THE INTERIOR OF THE MASK

Paint the interior of the mask with clear lacquer. This may seem inconsistent with the idea that the leather should absorb perspiration. Surprisingly enough, however, the mask will continue to "breathe."

The coatings of lacquer should be thin and penetrate deep into the leather. Use lacquer thinner to get a very thin consistency—thinner than you would use for spraying.

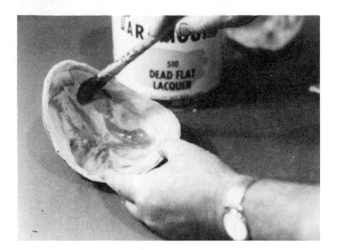

The lacquer dries so quickly that you can apply subsequent coatings almost immediately. The first application seals the surface of the leather, so the penetration is not deep on the second and third coats and the paint begins to build up.

Lacquer dries to a very hard finish, and it is likely that it will stiffen loose bits of leather, making them abrasive. The lacquered interior may need to be sanded to remove roughness. Use very fine (400 grit) sandpaper. The sanded spots should be coated one more time with clear lacquer.

COLORING THE LEATHER MASK

Always save some of the scraps that you trim from the mask as it is being made. You should test dyes on these scraps to get an indication of how they will take on the mask. You cannot use just any scrap of leather for this test. The dyes react differently on leather taken from the shoulder than on a piece from the belly. Two different leathers are likely to react differently depending on the tanning lot used. Finally, the pounding, rubbing, and polishing that *you* do to the leather will affect how it takes the dyes.

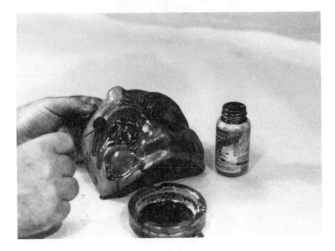

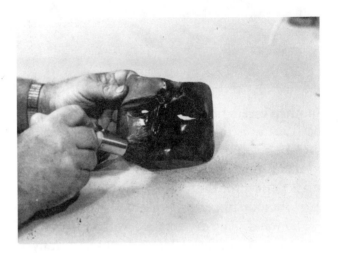

You can add a finish to your mask with the same dye and techniques that you would use to dye a pair of shoes. Use the applicator that comes with the dye or a stencil brush to apply the color. Spread the dye with small circular strokes of the brush. Leather-crafts stores have a wide assortment of colors that sound like they belong on leather—russet, sandal, buckskin, cordovan, etc., but they also come in greens, reds, blues, and yellows.

A shaving brush makes a very good applicator for applying the dyes. Work quickly, and buff the color as soon as you have an even coating. Start with a light tone of your color and then, if you want it darker, add another application of the dye.

Highlights and shadows can be added with an airbrush. The shadows (sprayed into the deeper recesses) can simply be a darker tone of dye. You will have to use a pigmented paint to make the highlights. If you want to put pigmented colors instead of dyes on the face of the mask, or you want to add colored accents to the features, be assured that leather receives paint very well. Lacquer, enamel, and acrylic paints take to leather with no problem.

Another excellent way to provide highlights to the features is to remove some of the dark dye. The abrasive powder contained in cleaners such as Ajax is finer than even the finest sandpapers, and is perfect for this process. Just a little picked up with your finger in a dry cloth is sufficient. Use no water. The dry abrasive works remarkably fast. (Yes, Ajax is available and is used in Italy.)

When you have the color you desire, you can seal the surface with a wax shoe polish (brown, black, or neutral) to give the leather a luster. No further sealer or coating is needed or recommended on the face of the mask.

Liquid Asphaltum

Art stores that cater to printing and the graphic arts sell a product that is variously known as "Liquid Asphaltum" or "Judean Pitch." This product is made of pitch (a thin solution of tar). It is manufactured to be used in the process of etching printing plates. Remarkably, it also

makes a very good stain for leather. It is easy to use and you have a high degree of control, not so much in the hue as in the darkness or value of the color. The asphaltum has a syrupy consistency and should be further thinned with naphtha or kerosene.

Apply the liquid asphaltum with a circular motion of your brush. The shaving brush works very well in this operation.

As soon as the asphaltum has been spread, begin to remove the surplus with a rag dipped in naphtha, kerosene, or white gas. A thin residue of pitch remains, which stains the leather to a light tone of brown.

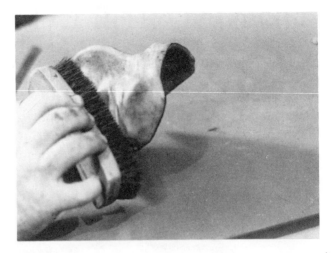

Buff the mask with a shoe brush. If the color is too light, wait for the stain to dry and give it another coating of the liquid asphaltum. Wipe off the surplus and buff the leather as you did before.

As a final touch, carefully paint the perimeter of the mask with dark brown or black dye.

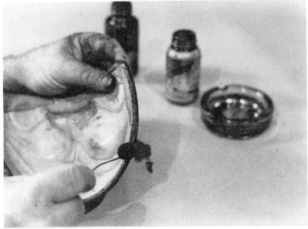

The eye holes should receive this same careful treatment of dark dye but, of course, you must wait for the eyes to be opened.

OPENING THE EYES OF A LEATHER MASK

You can cut leather with a pair of scissors, a sharp mat knife, or a sharp razor blade. The cutting edge of a wood chisel is also very effective. We have already demonstrated (page 157) how to shave paper thin leather tabs with the blade of a chisel. Now we will use this same chisel to cleanly open the eyes of the mask.

The eyes should be cut open as one of the last steps in the process of making a leather mask. If the eye is cut before the interior is lacquered and the mask has received its color, there is a great likelihood that the paints will run through the eye holes and mar the opposite side.

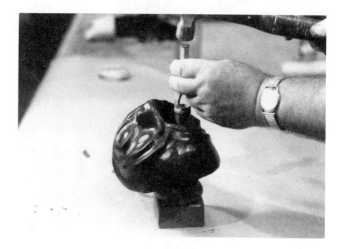

When cutting the eye hole, always back up the leather with a piece of soft wood. This banister knob is a good shape to reach up inside the mask and provide the necessary reinforcement. The chisel blade slices through the leather cleanly.

This hole-cutting chisel works very well on leather. Arlecchino's eyes are traditionally perfect circles, so this is the ideal tool for cutting his eyes. One or two blows of a hammer drive the cutter into the wood and through the leather.

The irregular shape of Brighella's eyes can be cut using the blade of this slightly curved wood chisel. Force one point of the blade into the corner of the eye and rock the handle forward, guiding the blade to follow the contour of the eye. The easy motion of this chisel slices a cut through the leather more cleanly than could ever be achieved with a knife blade.

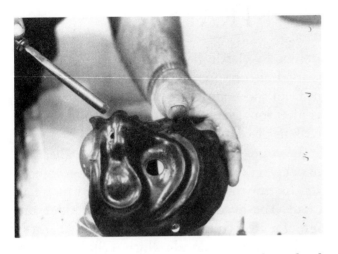

The edges around the eye holes should be dyed dark brown or black.

A curved chisel is the right tool for opening nose holes also. The cutting edge of the chisel must, of course, be small enough for the job.

MAKING HEAD STRAPS

The mask you build must be comfortably and securely attached to a performer's head. There must be no question that the mask might shift with head movement.

We were familiar with some masks that had been purchased in Italy. They had been fitted with leather straps, and we naturally assumed this was the standard, accepted method of attachment. When Ferruccio Soleri visited the U.S. in 1987, we spoke with him about the masks he used in performance. He scoffed at the leather strap, saying that it was built to satisfy the tourist trade rather than being designed for performance. He prefers an elastic band because it provides a gentle but continuous pressure as the posture of his head and body change in performance. Still, we offer you several alternatives for strapping your mask in place.

It's true. A set of leather straps on a leather mask gives the mask a good finished appearance. It's also true that every commedia character wears a hat. The head covering effectively hides any sign of a head strap, so no one can tell what it is made of. You can decide which technique serves you best.

Leather Straps

Once a leather strap is adjusted for the performer's head size, the mask will slip on and off without any further fussing with the buckle.

In making the leather straps you will be using three of those leather-working tools that you can only find at a leather-crafts store: a strip-cutting gauge, a hole punch, and a rivet set. (If you buy some ½ inch straps, you won't even need the cutter.)

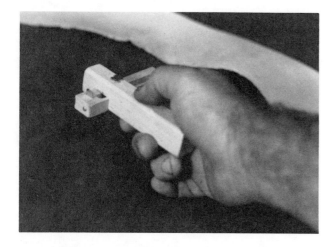 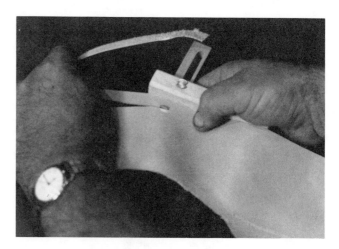

The strip-cutting gauge consists of a wooden handle and an adjustable wooden arm. A razor blade has been installed in the arm, running parallel to the handle. The arm is adjustable so straps of varying widths can be cut. As you pull a sheet of leather through the cutter, the inside edge slides along the handle and the blade cuts a strap with uniform width. Use 3 to 4 oz. leather, ½ inch brass buckles, and ¼ inch leather rivets to make the straps.

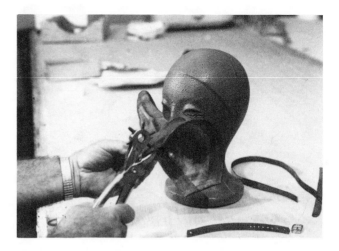

If you want leather straps on your mask, have them ready as you add color. The straps should be treated at the same time you dye the mask.

Use a hole punch to make ⅛ inch holes in the mask and the straps. You need a hole in one end of each strap to rivet it to the mask. The buckle side of the strap needs an elongated hole to accept the tongue of the buckle, and a pair of holes to rivet the strap to the buckle.

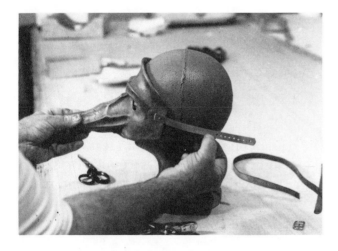

Measure the length of the strap with the mask on a head form (or a real head) and cut the strap to the correct length. Punch a series of ⅛ inch holes, about ½ inch apart, in the end of the strap for adjustment.

The rivets we are using in the illustrations come in two parts; a pin about ⅜ inch long, and a shorter piece called a cap. The pin fits inside the mask. It is inserted in the strap and then through the body of the mask. The cap slides over the pin and is forced firmly on the pin with a rivet set and a hammer.

The rivet set has a concave cup that fits snugly over the rivet. Two or three blows from a small hammer force the cap firmly onto the pin, and the leather pieces are securely anchored. Make sure you work on a solid base when you rivet. However, an anvil this large is not necessary.

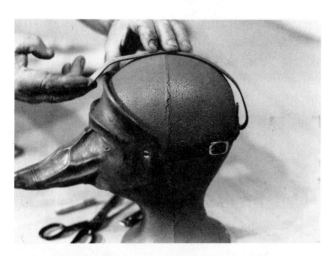

If you feel it is desirable, you can add another strap over the crown of the head. You can make the rear attachment with a rivet, but if you placed one in the front of the mask, it would be a definite distraction.

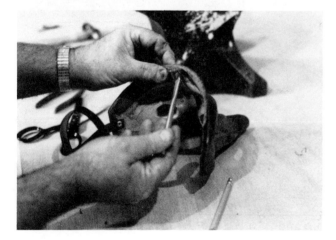

The tension on this strap is not great. Glue will hold it just fine. Lift a small section of the skived leather. Glue the strap with Barge cement, sandwiching it between the thin veneer of leather and the body of the mask.

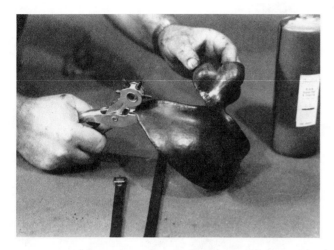

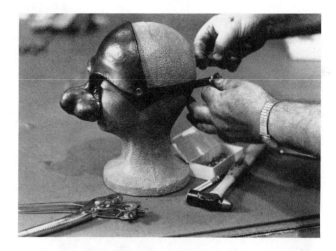

For most masks the correct placement of a head strap (no matter what material it is made of) is the balance point, behind the eye, just below the temple. The mask should be designed with a balance point in mind so a strap can be properly located.

Elastic Head Strap

We have used elastic as a head strap on several of the masks demonstrated in earlier parts of this book. The difference here is the method of attachment.

Fold the elastic band back over itself about ½ inch at the attachment point. Punch a hole that goes through both pieces of the fold. Reinforce the elastic with a small ½ inch leather washer you cut from a scrap piece of leather. Fix the elastic band to the body of the mask with a leather rivet.

Velcro Head Strap

This strap is made of two pieces of ⅝ inch cotton webbing. Sew two inches of Velcro to each of the strips of webbing. Measure your mask to the ac-

tor's head and cut the cloth straps to the correct length.

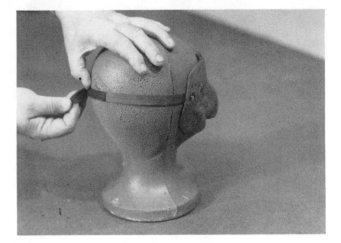

Fasten the strap to the temples of the mask with rivets and homemade leather washers, using the technique explained in attaching the elastic head strap.

The pressure applied to the mask is easily adjusted by the performer each time he puts the mask on. The tension on the connection is not great and Velcro is plenty strong enough to hold the mask securely.

ATTACHING FACE HAIR

A few of the commedia characters have hair growing from their faces. The earliest forerunners of Arlecchino had whiskers made of fur or horsehair. Pantalone traditionally has heavy gray eyebrows.

Brighella and Il Capitano sometimes (depending on which etching you refer to) possess bushy eyebrows.

Pantalone's Eyebrows

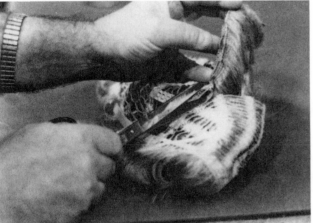

The eyebrow can be made of real hair by cutting up an old wig. Wigs are made by tightly binding real or artificial hair in ordered strips. The bands are then sewn to a skullcap made of netting. A few snips with a pair of scissors free up a very well organized row of hair exactly eyebrow width. A wig such as this can be expensive if purchased new, but fortunately, there is no need to buy it new. Wigs in a wide assortment of colors can be purchased in thrift shops.

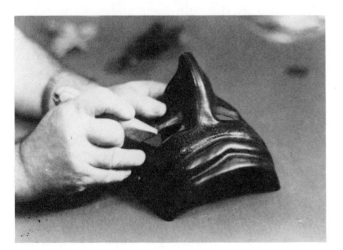

Make one slit about two inches long with a razor through the leather in the place where you want the eyebrow to grow. Cut a section from the row of hair to fill the razor slit. Feed a corner of the bound edge through the slit then, reaching under the mask, pull the strip into place.

If you use real hair, you can wet it and form it into shape just as you do your own hair. A hair curler is very effective. Artificial hair is more difficult, but hair spray helps to make it behave.

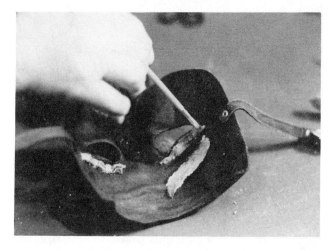

Use contact cement to glue the bound edge to the back of the mask. Neaten the appearance of the inside of the mask by gluing a skiving strip

over the raw edge of bound hair. When the glue is dry, lacquer the strip so it matches the mask interior.

Brighella's Moustache

The wool from a tanned sheepskin makes pretty good face hair for a mask. Examine the pelt to find a section that has the right length fleece. Working from the flesh side, cut a patch of fur

with a razor blade. The bushy hairs quickly spread as they leave the skin and almost hide their source.

If the cut edge of the skin is light colored and obvious, dye it dark with an application of the basic mask color.

Use contact cement to glue the fur patches to the upper lip of the mask.

Shape the fur to handlebars with a liberal application of styling gel.

If, however, you are content with gluing things to the front of the mask, you could use any of the standard makeup techniques employed by actors.

The same beard or mustache he sticks to his face with spirit gum could be applied to your mask.

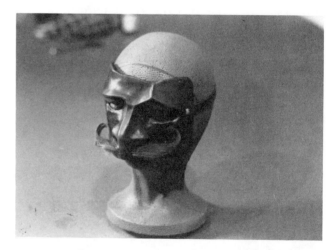

Brighella's mustache will be more realistic if you make it from real hair salvaged from a wig. One single row of hair, however, will not be bushy enough to do Brighella's mustache justice. The mask illustrated has been slit twice on each side. Two rows of bound hair were slipped into each

slit. Four rows of hair were thus installed on each side of his face in an attempt to make the mustache bushy enough.

We used hair styling gel and twirled the hair around a finger to make the curled ends.

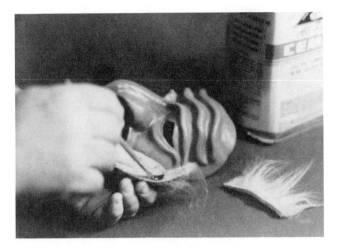

Pantalone's eyebrows could also be made from a section of white sheep's wool. Cut a long strip of fur with a razor blade, glue it to the mask with contact cement, and brush it straight.

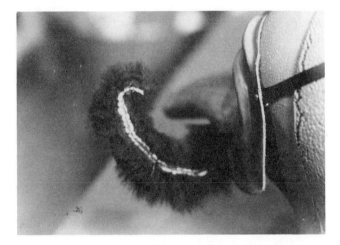

This long, exaggerated handlebar mustache for Il Capitano is also made from a strip of fur. The strip of fur is heavy. It has been tightly sewn to a thin wire for support and to keep the tips curled in the correct shape. The appliance is attached to the mask by sewing it through holes punched in the upper lip.

OTHER LEATHER-WORKING TECHNIQUES

*This photo shows the tools and workbench of a leather mask maker
in another studio in Venice, Italy.*

The Nature of Leather

Cowhides are made up of a tightly interlaced arrangement of microscopic protein fibers. Tiny spiraling cable-like cords join together, forming strands. These strands in turn form bundles, and the bundles interlock into a matrix. The network of tiny fibers is so interlocked that the skins of the bovine family are immensely strong. Leather will withstand repeated flexing, bending, and pulling without tearing. Tanned leather, although it no longer contains animal protein, retains this interlocked network. You can *stretch* vegetable tanned leather and *compress* it. This is the whole basis for being able to form leather over a positive form.

The side, shoulder, and back portions of a tanned cowhide are stiff and tough compared to the supple, narrow belly portion, but these can also be sculpted if you need the larger piece of leather. When you work with any part of the cowhide other than the belly you need to take a sterner approach in your techniques. A concentrated rubbing with the wooden sticketta is necessary, and this requires a lot of strength from your fingers and wrists. The problem all lies in the early stage of shaping, getting the wetted leather to conform reasonably close to the mask form, without having excessive webbing and folds develop. A leather press is very helpful (see below).

Once you get the leather forced into the correct beginning position, the final steps of pecking with the horn hammer and rubbing with the wooden stick are still good and appropriate techniques. The processes are not different from those explained on the preceding pages.

MAKING A LEATHER PRESS

A leather press consists of two gypsum cement molds—one positive and one negative. There is a uniform air space between the two molds of about 3/16 inch. A piece of leather pressed between these two forms finds that it just *must* eventually take the proper shape.

This animal face was designed by Bill Bathgate, and is so large that it cannot be molded from a piece of belly. It is amply large enough to illustrate the techniques of making and using a leather press. It was sculpted over a life mask, and was made to wear at The Renaissance Faire. The positive mold was cast in Hydrocal using the methods described in the section on Making a Positive Gypsum Cement Mold (page 79).

This mold is actually half of the press. We must, however, make another negative form. The first negative mold had no air space and, you will remember, was broken away in the "waste mold" process.

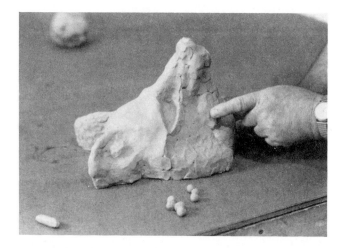

Roll a great number of little balls from modeling clay. You may need as many as two hundred (or more) of these ½ inch clay balls. One by one place each ball on the positive mold, and flatten it with your finger. Each ball should cover about ¾ inch of the surface and be about ⅛ to 3/16 inch thick.

As you get a section covered with these ¾ inch clay patches, rub the clay, blending the patches into a smooth blanket, which will be no more than ³/₁₆ inch thick.

You may be tempted to shortcut this somewhat tedious task of rolling, flattening, and blending the balls, thinking that a rolling pin would provide a much quicker blanket of clay of the right thickness. It would, but you would find that as the blanket is laid on the form it would stretch thin in places, and bunch up thickly in others. You will have the most uniform covering by making and manipulating these little balls of clay.

If you are modeling with an oil-based clay, put a little petroleum jelly on your fingertips to polish the surface and make it as smooth as you can get it. (If you use water-based clay, dip your fingertips in a little water for the needed lubrication.) The surfaces of both the positive and negative molds should be absolutely free of roughness so the leather can slide inside the press.

It is extremely important that all parts of your positive mold taper toward the tip of the nose. It would be most difficult to separate the halves of the press if there were any undercuts in the mask design.

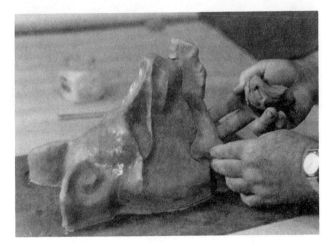

Build a clay wall around the lower border of the form. The mask ends at the nose and jowl, so the negative Hydrocal mold should terminate here too. The open side helps to make separation of the two halves easy.

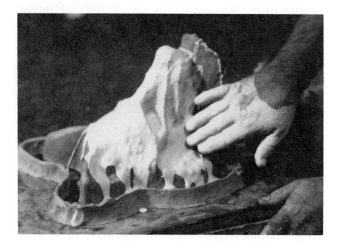

Proceed with the same techniques you used earlier, when you made your first negative mold. Mix a batch of casting material (not plaster, but Hydrocal this time), build a clay barrier around your mold, apply an impression coating, pile more of the mix on the form (to a thickness of at least 1½ inches), and set the casting aside to cure.

When the casting has cured, pry the halves apart. Remove all of the clay. You have your press—a positive mold and a negative shell with a consistent ³⁄₁₆ inch clearance between them, and you are now ready to shape some leather.

Select a cut of leather from the side or shoulder of a hide. Try to get this cut from the lower side of the skin. The shoulder and back are the toughest portions of the hide and are the most difficult to shape. Soak the leather in hot water for 10 to 15 minutes. Knead the saturated leather, roll it, wring it, and twist it to awaken the fibers. Use the strength of your fingers to force the leather into the outlines of the mold's surface. It won't behave, but do your best to have it your way.

Sandwich the wet leather between the two halves of the press. Try to retain the meager beginnings of the form that you were able to get with your fingers, as the two halves of the press are mated.

Turn the press over and give the positive mold several firm whacks with a rubber mallet. This helps to seat the pieces of the press, and forces the leather into the air gap.

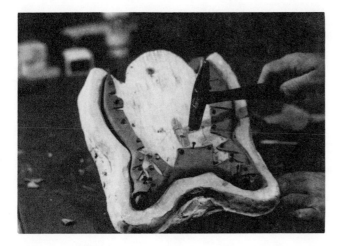

We bonded a piece of ¾ inch plywood to the base of the Hydrocal mold by drilling and pegging it. This allows us to tack the leather firmly to the mold.

Cover the mated press with several thicknesses of heavy, wet burlap to retard the drying of the leather. Put some fairly intense pressure on the two halves of the press. This pressure could be in the form of weight—sandbags or stage weights—or you could use clamps.

Let the press do its work on the leather for 2 to 3 hours. The interlacing fibrils are uncoiling and stretching a little bit, and slipping into new

homes within the matrix. This process cannot be made to happen immediately. It takes a little time.

When the press is opened, you will see that the features are beginning to take shape. The leather has also begun to dry out a little. It is no longer sloppy and saturated, but it is still very damp. Major stretching can be done with wet leather, but damp leather can be worked with a tool. Rub the leather hard with your tool, encouraging the fibers to take the new shape. After about 20 minutes of working with a tool, the features are much better defined.

Diligent vigorous rubbing in all directions — vertical, horizontal, and diagonal (especially rubbing into the depressions) — will begin to compress the network of fibrils forcing the leather close to the mold. A concentrated rubbing slowly but surely shapes the wet leather and smooths out all of the fullness that has gathered. It is remarkable how much rubbing and shaping leather will take without damage to its surface. Of course, your tools must not start to scrape, or they will make abrasions in the leather, which will soon do permanent damage.

These steps (pressing and rubbing) must be repeated several times. It would be redundant to show photographs illustrating the repetitions. Just do it.

Put the mask back into the press for another 2 to 3 hours. As the press is doing its stretching, the leather is still drying out.

Again rub the leather with your wooden tool. This can be strenuous work. The side portion of a cowhide is tough, and you must be unrelenting in your efforts.

Use the press again. You could even leave the leather in the press overnight.

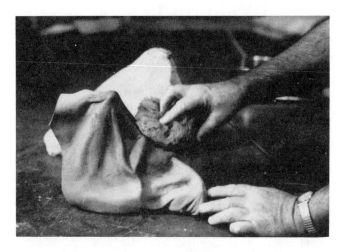

You might find it helpful to moisten the leather slightly in the small area you are working if it has dried out too much. If it needs to be a little wetter, a sponge will bring moisture to the right spot.

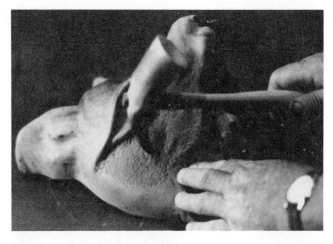

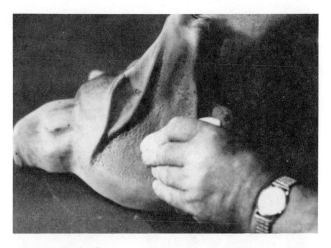

When the leather is finally lying reasonably close to the mold, finishing the shaping of the mask with techniques shown before. Peck at the surface with the horn hammer, and rub the surface smooth with the wooden tool.

Trim the mask, making your cut precisely on the line that you have chosen to be the mask's perimeter.

Paint the interior of the mask with three thin coatings of clear lacquer. Color the mask with leather dyes. We chose to use a cordovan dye for this wolf mask.

FINISHING THE PERIMETER OF THE MASK (EASY METHOD)

A mask made from the side section of a cowhide is very stable. You can finish the perimeter of the mask by following the steps of embedding a wire in the border, as outlined earlier. Or you can use this alternative, simpler method, employing an "edge bevel," beeswax, and an "edge slicker."

An edge bevel cleans up saw-toothed snags and loose fibers left by the scissors. It has a very small chisel placed between two pronged guides. As the tool is pushed along the leather, the guides keep everything aligned, and the chisel point cuts a slight bevel from the leather's edge. Running the tool along the other side of the edge puts a slight bevel there too, and the edge becomes uniformly rounded.

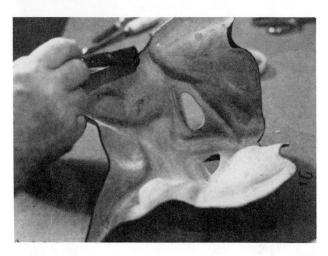

Very carefully paint the rounded edge with a coating of black dye. If you don't want to use black that's fine, but choose some dark color.

Coat the painted edge with beeswax. Rub the wax back and forth on the leather's edge.

An edge slicker is a wheel with a groove cut into its rim. It can be made of either wood or plastic. The slicker is designed to be vigorously rubbed along the waxed edge of a piece of thick leather to burnish it. The tool forces the wax into the grain of the leather along this edge and polishes it, giving it a fine, finished appearance.

This is the finished mask being worn by the designer.

COLORING A LEATHER MASK
WITH PIGMENTED PAINTS

All paints adhere very well to the surface of leather. Enamel, lacquer, or acrylic paints could be used to highlight and accent a leather mask. But one of the best features of leather is its appearance when it is in its natural state or when it is treated with dyes. If you cover your mask with an agent other than dye, you might just as well have crafted it from some other material, as far as the appearance is concerned.

There are reasons other than appearance to consider: leather is lightweight, it is easily fitted, comfortable in a variety of ways, and it is durable. So you may be excused for putting pigmented paints on your leather mask if the designer feels that it is appropriate.

Making a Smooth Finish on Leather

Leather can be sanded to make it as smooth as an automobile finish. If it is not flexed excessively, the finish can be polished to a high gloss. There are just a few rules to follow to obtain this gloss.

Use very fine sandpaper, grit #300 or even the finer grit #400—the kinds that are designed to be used in preparing an automobile for lacquer paint. This sandpaper is intended to be used with water. Of course, we cannot use water on the mask. Water acts as a lubricant, and keeps the very fine grit from getting clogged with the debris obtained from the abrasions, in this case, leather dust. Sand very lightly, in a circular motion. This helps to keep the paper clear. In the absence of water, however, the paper *will* get clogged. As the sandpaper becomes loaded with waste matter rotate it to find a new area where the grit is clean and sharp.

When you have sanded the surface smooth— that is to say, when you decide to stop sanding in the belief that the surface is truly as smooth as it can be, and you are not just bored with the process—give the mask a prime coat of paint.

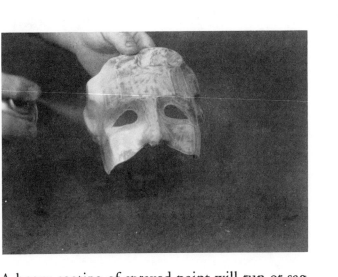

Spray on several light coats of white lacquer undercoat. Do not brush the paint, or you will lose the smoothness to the marks left by your brush.

A heavy coating of sprayed paint will run or sag and again you will lose the smoothness you sanded so long to achieve.

When the paint has dried overnight, you can sand it again. This time your sandpaper will be clogged with paint. Be patient, sand gently, with a circular motion, and keep changing the paper.

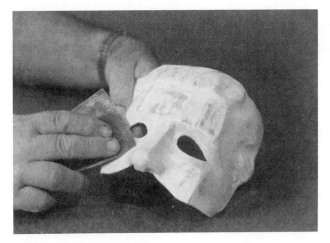

You are now working very much like an auto body refinisher. Sand gently, concentrating on the high spots on the mask. Sand the corners very little. Do not sand away *all* of the white prime coat. It is to your advantage to leave a thin coat of the paint in the depressions. It helps to even the surface, making the skin as flat as possible.

If you have done a good job of sanding the mask is ready for its finish coating of paint—any color. We chose to use white on this neutral half mask.

APPENDIX

GLOSSARY

Acetone. A solvent used to dissolve paints, fats, and plastic resins.

Alginate. A mold-making material formulated from kelp. It has excellent reproductive properties and is non-toxic. It is the only mold-making material that is safe to use against human skin.

Asphaltum. A thinned solution of pitch or tar. Mask makers use this liquid as a stain for leather.

Belly. A narrow portion of leather cut from the underside of a tanned cowhide. Belly is very flexible, easily tooled, and recommended for making masks.

Casting. A reproduction made from an original pattern or any mold.

Celastic. A trade name for a casting material made of plastic-filled fabric.

Chasing. A technique of forming and ornamenting sheet metal by hammering a pattern in its front surface with blunt tools.

Commedia dell'arte. A technique of performing a story, which originated in Italy in the mid 16th century. The scenario was outlined, but not scripted. The performers improvised the words and actions.

Edge bevel. A leather-working tool consisting of a chisel edge set between two guides and mounted in a handle. It is designed to trim roughness and unevenness from the edge of a piece of leather.

Edge slicker. A leather-working tool consisting of a narrow, concave groove cut into a piece of plastic or hardwood. The tool is rubbed (with a hard wax) over the border of a leather mask, after it has been trimmed with a an edge bevel, to further smooth the exposed edge.

Flesh side. A term to distinguish between the front and back of a piece of leather. The flesh side is what we would usually consider to be the back side of a piece of leather — the part that was next to the meat and flesh of the animal.

Friendly Plastic. A trade name for a low temperature thermoplastic of the polyolefin family. The product is packaged in the form of rice-sized grains which soften when dropped in hot water. The resulting taffy-like plastic can be shaped and cast in a negative mold.

Grain side. The outer layer (hair side) of a piece of tanned leather.

Gypsum cement. A cement made of gypsum, which works a lot like its cousin plaster (also made of gypsum) but is much different in its chemistry. It is harder and stronger than plaster.

Hexcelite. A trade name for a plastic orthopaedic tape. It was designed to be used by doctors to set broken bones, but can be used to make stylized masks and costumes.

Horn hammer. A leather-working tool so specialized that you must make it yourself. The head of the hammer is a cow horn. The pointed end is used to peck repeatedly at a moistened leather surface, forcing it to conform to the shape of an underlying mold.

Hydrocal. A trade name for one formulation of gypsum cement.

Latex rubber. A liquid made from the secretions of rubber plants. Flexible rubber reproductions can be cast with this liquid in a plaster mold.

Leather press. A press consisting of two molds: a positive form and a negative form with a carefully predetermined space between them. It is helpful in shaping tough portions of a side of leather.

Life mask. A reproduction of the face of a living person. There are two steps in the process; a negative casting is taken from the face in alginate, then a positive plaster casting is taken from the alginate.

Liquid asphaltum. *See* **asphaltum.**

Mask. 1. A face covering. 2. The face covering, costume, posture, gestures, actions, and attitude that make up the persona of a character.

Masque. 1. A dramatic performance popular during the 16th and 17th centuries in England. 2. A piece written for such a performance.

Mold. A pattern from which a casting is taken.

Mold release. A thin coating applied to the face of a mold to ensure that the casting will not adhere to the mold's surface.

Mother mold. A firm, close-fitting cradle used to support a flexible mold, forcing it to retain a true shape.

Naphtha. A petroleum distillate used as a thinner for paint or varnish.

Negative mold. A form that displays the features of a three-dimensional object in reverse relief. A negative form of a face would show the nose and chin as deep hollows.

Neoprene casting rubber. A synthetic rubber designed to replace latex. Neoprene is available in liquid form, which can be used to make mask castings in a negative plaster mold.

Persona. The personality of a character assumed by an actor.

Plasticine. A trade name for non-drying modeling clay. Its plasticizer may be based in oil or wax.

Polyolefin. Any of a family of thermoplastics including polyethylene, polypropylene, and ethyl vinyl acetate. Friendly Plastic and hot glue are products from the polyolefin family.

Positive mold. A mold that contains the features of a three-dimensional object in their original relationships. The mold has a realistic likeness to its prototype.

Release agent. *See* **mold release.**

Repoussé. A technique of shaping and ornamenting sheet metal by hammering a pattern in its reverse side with blunt end tools.

Rivet set. A tool for setting rivets. Mask makers use the tool to rivet head straps to leather masks.

Skiving tool. A leather-working tool which shaves thin strips from the flesh side of a piece of leather.

Sticketta. A leather-working tool made of a piece of wood about 4 to 5 inches long. It is used in forming and polishing leather masks.

Tanning. A process whereby animal skins are chemically altered to become leather.

Thermoplastics. A broad classification of plastics which soften when they are exposed to heat. They can be shaped and when they are cooled they solidify, retaining their new form.

Vizard. A small mask that covers only the area around the eyes.

Waste mold. A mold (usually made of plaster) that must be destroyed in order to release it from its casting.

WHERE TO GET YOUR SUPPLIES

You will be using a wide variety of vendors as you purchase your supplies for mask making. In the following list, we first suggest headings in your telephone book's Yellow Pages, so you can make your purchases locally. If you are not successful in the phone book, we suggest vendors we work with who do mail order business (most are in the Los Angeles area). Call them to verify prices, availability, payment method, etc.

Alginate
"Dental Supplies"
or
Davis Dental Supply
North Hollywood, CA
(213) 875-3040
(This business caters to the entertainment industry.)

Metal sheets: aluminum, brass, copper
"Metals" or "Aluminum," "Brass," etc.

Chasing tools
"Jewelry Supplies"
or
J. F. McCaughin Co.
Rosemead, CA
(800) 255-9271

Roofing tar
"Roofing Supplies"

Casting Plaster
#1 pottery plaster
Gypsum cement
Hydrocal
"Ceramics Supplies"
or
United States Gypsum
(800) 621-9523

Latex rubber
Neoprene
R&D Latex Corp.
City of Commerce, CA
(213) 724-6161

Solvents: acetone, naphtha
Sandpaper (400 grit)
"Painter's Supplies" or "Automotive Paint Supplies"

Elastic
Velcro
Millinery wire
"Sewing Supplies" or "Millinery"
or
California Millinery
Los Angeles, CA
(213) 622-8746

Hexcelite
"Medical Supplies (Orthopedics)"
or
Douglas & Sturgess Medical Supp.
San Francisco, CA
(415) 421-4456
(A company that does a lot of business with sculptors.)

Friendly Plastic
"Theater and Stage Supplies"
or
Friendly Plastic
2888 Bluff St. #233
Boulder, CO 80301
(Write for inquiries; this company discourages phone calls.)

Celastic
"Theater and Stage Supplies"
or
Alcone Company, Inc.
Long Island City, NY
(718) 361-8373

Hot glue
"Craft Supplies"
or
Adhesive Machinery (Hysol)
Sea Brook, NH
(603) 474-5541

Flex glue
Spectra Dynamics
Albuquerque, NM
(505) 843-7202
(Phlexglu)

Gold leaf
Modeling clay
"Artist Supplies"

Metallic tapes
"Tape"
or
Southwestern Bag Co.
Los Angeles, CA
(213) 622-6108

Leather
Leather tools: skive, edge bevel, edge slicker, rivet set
Barge cement
Animal furs
"Tannery" or "Leather Crafts Supplies"
or
Tandy Leather Company
(stores nationwide)
Headquarters: Fort Worth, TX
(817) 244-6404

Asphaltum
Judean pitch
"Printer's Supplies (Graphics)"
or
LA Arts Supply
West Los Angeles, CA
(213) 312-6680

BIBLIOGRAPHY

There are not many books on the subject of mask making—certainly very few in print. The following list is not extensive, but I have been searching and these are the ones I have found and researched in writing this book. Many magazine articles have been published.

Acting Experiences with Masks

Behind the Mask, by Bari Rolfe. Oakland, CA: Personabooks, 1977.

Mask Characterization by Libby Appel. Carbondale, IL: Southern Illinois University Press, 1982.

Ethnic Masks

There are many books in print on regional masks of various countries, interpreting their use and meaning. Most are profusely illustrated, many are in color. I have not attempted to collect these works.

No/Kyogen Masks—and Performance, compiled by Rebecca Teele. Claremont, CA: Mime Journal, Pomona College Theater, 1984.

I Am Not Myself: The Art of African Masquerade, edited by Herbert M. Cole. University of California, Museum of Cultural History, Monograph Series, Number 26.

Sculpture Techniques

Sculpture—Principles and Practice, by Louis Slobodkin, 1949. Mineola, NY: Dover Publications, Inc., rereleased 1973.

Commedia dell'Arte

Commedia dell'Arte—A Scene Study Book, by Bari Rolfe. Oakland, CA: Personabooks.

The Italian Comedy, by Pierre Louis Ducharte, 1929. Translated from the French by Randolph Weaver. Mineola, NY: Dover Publications, Inc., rereleased 1966.

Working with Leather

Leatherwork Manual, by Al Stohlman, A. D. Patten, J. A. Wilson. Tandy Leather Company, 1969–84.

Leathercraft, by Sid Latham. New York: Winchester Press, 1977.

The Book of Buckskinning (Vols. I, II, III, IV), edited by William Scurlock. Rebel Publishing Co., 1981.

Leather Masks

These books by Donato Sartori are profusely illustrated with sketches and photographs (almost all in color) of the leather sculptures (mostly masks) of Donato and his father Amleto. The text is in Italian, but the photographs transcend language barriers.

Arte della maschera nella Commedia dell'Arte, by Donato Sartori and Bruno Lanata, 1983

This book traces the history of commedia from its beginnings to the present day productions in Italy. 204 pages, 250 illustrations.

Rito e mito della maschera, L'opera dei Sartori, 1987

A cross-section of multicultural masks with an emphasis on the masks and other sculptures of the Sartoris. 124 pages, 258 illustrations.

Maschera e Maschere, by Donato Sartori and Bruno Lanata, 1984

A "how-to" book on crafting masks. There is an emphasis on making the mask in leather. 110 pages, 222 illustrations.

The Commedia dell'Arte, and the masks of Amleto and Donato Sartori, by Alberto Marcia, 1980

This book is in English but is published and distributed in Italy. 66 pages, 174 illustrations

The only way I know of obtaining these books is to order directly from Sartori's school and museum in Padua, Italy.

Centro Maschere e Strutture Gestuali
Via Cesare Battisti n 191
35031 Albano Terme
Padova, Italia

INDEX